A Key to the Grove
and Other Poems

Peter Coe Verbica

A Key to the Grove
and Other Poems

"Owl" © 2010 Melissa West.

"...rendered with beautiful and arresting figurative language."

Ron Hanson, author of *Desperadoes and Mariette in Ecstasy*

Peter Coe Verbica

Praise for Verbica's poetry

"These are terrific poems, by turns romantic and comic, confessional and descriptive. Each offering is wise, surprising, authentic, and rendered with beautiful and arresting figurative language. I have rarely read a collection that I could say was entertaining, but Peter Coe Verbica has accomplished that with his keen eye, huge heart, and wit."

Ron Hansen, Author of *Desperadoes, Mariette in Ecstasy, Hitler's Niece.*

"Most of us wrestle with one demon or another, and Peter Verbica is no exception. But his demons lie in wait inside his well-crafted and deceptively homespun poems. After we enter and pass through his personal darkness, the sun seems to finally rise over him. The language snaps like branches in winter, crackles like firelight, and finally washes down like summer rain."

Greg Pliska, Composer

"What is poetry but an invitation for us to take risks? That's what I enjoy best about Peter Verbica's work. He doesn't scold humanity for being dishonest. He knows that no one would listen. Instead, he uses his poetic license to be open about his own feelings, no matter how raw or unrefined. Peter plays upon his audience's heartstrings with unflinching sincerity and grace. His poems will lift your spirits, encourage you to question and may inspire you to find the divine in the most ordinary."

> The Rev. Steve Privett, S.J.
> President, University of San Francisco

"Peter Coe Verbica's A KEY TO THE GROVE allows us to witness the perceptions and hesitations of a lively contemporary mind in unfettered fluency and fluidity. There should be a law, we think, against writing so well with such easy-going fecundity. Each poem's twists and turns struck this reader as simultaneously unexpected and inevitable. Never heavy-handed, always open to the spontaneous revisions of experience, Verbica allows us to grow with him as he skeptically surveys the world as he finds it. The book is unusually handsome visually as well as verbally. What fountains forth here in one of our local poets can only be admired and envied."

Vito Victor, author of "Desert Song"

"Original and inventive."

Maggie Paul, author of *Borrowed World*

"A great collection of poems!! His poems were so intense and vivid that you could feel his emotions. Some of his love poems were a little gut wrenching and hard to finish as they evoked your own memories of love. It was as if you were looking into his soul. This is a great little book to have in your collection."

Melissa Menser Scarpace, Teacher, Member of the popular Santa Cruz Roller Derby Girls, reviewing Verbica's *Greece at Peace*.

Dedicated to
my daughters

(four only children
who happened
to grow up in the
same household)

and to my wife, Tiffany,
who taught me
that the best poem
is the one which we live.

"Ай да Пушкин, ай да сукин сын!"

"Way to go, Pushkin! Way to go, you son-of-a-bitch!"

Alexander Pushkin

A Key to the Grove and Other Poems

© 1998-2013 Peter Verbica

ISBN: 978-0-9911535-1-0 [print edition]

All rights reserved. No parts of this publication may be reproduced, stored in a retrieval system or transmitted in any form or by any means, electronic, mechanical, photocopies, recording or otherwise, without the prior written consent of the author.

˜ *First Printing* ˜

"Castrojeriz,""Wind and Rain,""Relic," "Vierge d'Orisson,""Burden," "Stray Dog," "Storks Azofra," and "Pilgrim Feet," © 2007 Melissa West. All rights reserved. Used with permission of the artist.

"Owl" © 2010 Melissa West. All rights reserved. This book's cover graphics and title page utilizing the "Owl" was modified by author with permission of Ms. West.

"Reception" photo after title page © 2012 Lindsey Gonzales. Used with permission. Modified by the author with permission of Ms. Gonzales.

"Wedding Bed" photo © 2012 Justin Doward. Used with permission.

Owl coin logo on last page and ladder and shield heraldry on this page © Getty Images.

Published by
Peter Coe Verbica
Santa Cruz, California

Table of Contents

Greece at Peace 2
A Pair of Good Boots 9
The Barn House 11
Sleep 18
Laughter Jumps 20
Contours 22
Sufi in the Sandstorm 26
Bullets of Rain 30
Doves at Dawn 32
120 Degrees of Separation 35
Bicycles 37
Running Buddha 39
Artist 41
Natural Bridges 43
A Séance in Silver 48
A New Blue Suit 54
Wedding Bed 58
Diamond Ring 60
48 62
Jean-Paul 64
A Rain of Rice 77
Style 79
Christmas 82
A Day before Christmas 90
Hakone 98
Paris and Milan 101
The Ascension 104
To My Friends 110
Mysterious Initials 113
The Wet Wheel 116

Beyond Your Blue Eyes	126
Piano Climbing	128
Tennis	133
The Perfect Place	134
The Table	137
Conversations of Touch	139
Horses in Motion	143
Parachute	146
Breaking Windows	149
Colors of Koi	153
In the Morning	154
A Spider in the Sun	155
Sandals on My Feet	156
Ghosts in the Cold	157
Gone	159
Pretty Songs	160
The Bridge	161
Easter Riddles	169
Gateway to a Dream	174
One Word	179
An Honest Afternoon	180
The Hat Miracle	185
Magnificent Sadness	193
A Brief Ode to Crossfit	195
Peace of Immortality	198
Simple Sunlight	199
This Town	202
Coyotes in the Canyon	205
Dear Vanessa	207
Joseph	211
Bare Hands	215
I grew up	218
Tombstone of a Town	226

The Flakes..230
Pants of the Dead 234
Happy Birthday...236
A Day of Ordinary Thinking......................................238
The Sidewalk Sale 242
The Last Magazine...246
Pilgrimage 249
Iron Woman..254
Happy Anniversary...257
A Key to the Grove 261
Beat by Beatniks 266
We Could Talk..270
A Beautiful Ballerina 276
A Road Trip Resolution 287

Artwork and Photographs

"Castrojeriz" 8
"Wind and Rain"..29
"Relic" 34
"Vierge d'Orisson" 47
"Burden" 53
"Wedding Bed" 57
"Stray Dog" 158
"Storks Azofra" 237
"Pilgrim Feet" 248
"Owl" 260

Greece at Peace
1999

Simple buildings,
warm and white,
hang like fresh towels above the harbor.

Foreign voices
I begin to recognize:
as if awaking from
a twenty-five year slumber:

They are my emotions.

(I meander and recount
the steps that you took to get
to the water.

Do you remember the
whole village watching
you?)

I still have the photograph
of us on the dock.
You touched my ear
with your tongue
just before the click
of the shutter.

You would chuckle:

I keep thinking of
your sleepy straw hat:

And, of course,

A Key to the Grove and Other Poems
~Peter Coe Verbica~

your smile underneath,
which you would hide
like a puppy in
a basket.

I see your dark glasses
hanging fearlessly on your nose:

like a carefree diver.

I sat in our cafe,
though the owner passed
away last year.

I gave his wife two hugs:
one from me and one
from you.

She scolded me for being
with you and said,
"You knew that she was too pretty
for it to last."
I answered with a grin, "I know. I know."

I pour my light heart
into a porcelain cup
and think of your sugar.

I am writing down everything
that I should forget:
I am a historian to my own
dementia.

Remember gliding past me
on a bicycle? You had a

loaf of bread balanced on the handle bars
and a hint of a swimsuit.

(You forgave me for insisting that
you join a local circus.
I forgave you for chasing me around
in a ring as if I was a bear.)

I spend the rest of the afternoon
running after your mirage:

which in a tribute to apostolic
succession,

reappears around each
whitewashed stairwell.

(Your presence was betrayed
with a kiss before
I got up this morning.)

I am sad to report that the cottage
which we leased is now
full of chocolatines and caramel
and round tables.

I am in the house on the hill:
the one that you loved looking at
after the sun's sequester.

I sit on the terrace
and the moon laughs
at me like an old Greek
proudly showing off
his gold teeth.

A Key to the Grove and Other Poems
~Peter Coe Verbica~

A neighbor plays a
gypsy's violin on his
porch as if out of a postcard.
I swear that it is strung
with his family's tears.
The music taunts
your memory out
from under the olive trees.

I translate his song
using a ship captain's
quill
and thin airmail paper:

"When your boat
went out to sea,
and left me with
the child of your
memory...

You left your name
burnt into me.

I waited and wondered,
as if for an eternity.

How could I know
that in another
lifetime,
you would come back?

Please don't torture
me with what could be.

Leave. I've spent

too many years
reading you reading me."

For some reason, it reminds
me of a painting in
a children's book:

the one of an Owl, a Pussycat,
and a Tropical Fish in a bowl.

I wish the blue ocean,
with its comfortable waves,
was your denim jeans
at the base of our bed.

I wish the afternoon
would open,
like your favorite
cotton shirt.

I wish that we could
happily bounce forward:

you feeling the keel
as it holds you fast in deep water.

Let me set sail for a favorite cove.
Let the coast become a
visible innuendo:
effortlessly arching backwards
into a beautiful crescent.

Come dive with me into the future:
ahead of the power boats and nets:

We will give away Neptune's fortune:

A Key to the Grove and Other Poems
~Peter Coe Verbica~

a treasure of silver spheres
which rise towards the surface.

Your eyes will be the compass
by which we navigate ecstasy.

Your hands above your head
tell me the time on
your clock:

I remember the wringing
of each chime
and it takes its toll.

© 2007 by Melissa West.

A Pair of Good Boots
2009

Fear is nothing more
than a rickety fence,
a lean-to of brittle yesterdays.

Courage easily vaults over it –
if we let up on the reins,

and raise ourselves
slightly above the saddle.

Lean forward in life!
It will help you keep your balance.

Smile discretely
as you pass over
the obstacles
which hemmed you in,

and whether your goal
is time or form,
keep looking ahead.

Count the paces
to yourself,

and be ready for
the next jump or river.

You are upon
nearly one thousand pounds
of moving muscle.

And, if you fall,
for whatever reason,
roll away.

Remember,
the dirt is usually softer
than you imagine.

Brush yourself off
and give a loose and friendly wave.

(You're passing on a piece
of your courage to others
and getting more back in return.)

One last thing before I forget: spoil yourself
with a pair of good boots.

They are like two trusted friends,
who help you avoid danger when you are
thrown.

A Key to the Grove and Other Poems
~Peter Coe Verbica~

The Barn House
2009

Let me apologize
from the outset:

if the
fruit of
my writing

produces
the seeds of
poems within poems:

for at times
the heartache
and happiness
inside me

spill out
like glistening
black pearls

as if from a
redolent papaya:

leaving
soft, sweet slivers
upon one's lips:

at best
like the kisses from
a lost lover

who is finally found.

Let me apologize from the
outset for my
autobiography,

when I tell you of
a woman and a wife
in my life for two decades

who asked me
out of her world
with a long goodbye.
At first, in shock,
I prayed
in an adobe chapel,
my knees upon Mexican pavers.

I cried in dark theatres
and listened to sad songs,
and drove slowly through
the outskirts of town.

I pleaded with patient priests
and begged a God Whom
I didn't know well for a miracle.

I wore shame like a sweater
until finally overcome with the heat:

I tore it off as if struck by a fever
and ran naked into the rain:

mad with anguish.

Have you ever been
stripped of everything

A Key to the Grove and Other Poems
~Peter Coe Verbica~

and brought down to bare wood?

For months,
I was torn down

stick by stick,
wire by wire,
stone by stone,

taken apart
like a war-torn village:

Nothing was sacred
to the occupier.

Every revered memory
was unearthed
and the gold teeth removed,
one by one,
from each smile.

The heart
of every dream
shared together
was burnt out.

My insides
were charred
and drew into itself
as if charcoal:

leaving me the
embodiment of a crude canoe.

So, I let myself go

into
the rolling river
of life
and floated for miles,

until I found a pristine shore.

I pulled myself from the water:
Baptized and cleansed
from anger and remorse:

over round stones
and walked up through
the tall grass
to a hillside of green.

I overlooked the rapids
and sat in the sun.

The sound was soothing
and I thought:

> *It is as if I*
> *have emerged from a crash*
> *which I couldn't prevent*
> *despite every effort:*
>
> *Somehow my parachute*
> *opened in the descent and I am*
>
> *Like a lone pilot walking*
> *in slow motion:*
>
> *Away from the wreckage*
> *of what was*
> *a beautiful*
> *flying machine.*

A Key to the Grove and Other Poems
~Peter Coe Verbica~

>*I leave it smoking in the desert:*
>
>*A spiral works its way into the skyline:*
>*A black smudge branding the Appaloosa*
>*of blue, white, and gray.*
>
>*I am here with bloodshot eyes:*
>*dirty and bruised,*
>*but not broken.*
>
>*(This was my old image*
>*And then there is the birth of a new one:*
>
>*like a rapture.)*

I have an overwhelming
Desire to build a new
And sturdy house:

Tall and strong like my four daughters.

I've been thinking about
its foundation,
insulation
and finish.

I have been thinking of a saw's teeth
through fresh wood
and the release of a claw hammer's energy
upon the heads of 12 penny nails.

This house:

let us make it board and batten
and brown

like a barn:

With high ceilings
and the galley open
to the dining and living room:

A large hearth,
big and warm
like my new heart.

I want to talk with a
specialist in heating and air conditioning,
and another about life off of the grid.

I want over-sized paintings
and simply-framed photographs
and subtle lighting

to bring an aura to each vignette.

Perhaps the house can be set back
and sheltered from neighbors:
I no longer care about what the outside
thinks.

This house is my soul.

and the olive trees which I plant
along the long driveway
will be its guardian angels.

I will ring a brass ship's bell
which hangs near the loft's doors.

And my children and I
will sit at a rough-hewn table

made smooth and oiled with our own hands:

and our laughter will
be the prayers
which we offer
as Thanksgiving

for our barefoot and blue jean moments
spent together.

Sleep
2009

Sleep like Chagall.

Rest
in a quilted sky

above a quiet sea.

Close
your starry eyes
and reach your arms

through the gossamer
of the sky.

Grab
a sterling cloud for a pillow

and nuzzle
next to the moon.

Let a warm tropical rain
play a lullaby
on thin tin roofs.

Kiss me
for part of eternity.

Whisper
to me in French,

and I will translate
your words
in my dreams.

A Key to the Grove and Other Poems
~Peter Coe Verbica~

Let us sail over chains of islands.

Promise
that you will wake up
naked next to me,

and stretch as if we were just borne,

breathing in the night,
breathing out our light.

Laughter Jumps
© 2009 by Peter Verbica

On the edge of land,
we stand,
like two cypress trees
intertwined above the sand.

Arm in arm,
Hand in hand,
following a trail cut
into the cliff,
a winding strand.

The salt of the sea
is upon our lips,
the grass in waves
nearly to our hips.

Later in the day,
from a rooftop café:

our laughter jumps
from the window
and dives into the Bay.

If gulls could talk,
what would they say,
gliding above our sadness and
the ocean's spray.

Out of place,
we feel God's embrace:

A setting sun
at the end of the day,

A Key to the Grove and Other Poems
~Peter Coe Verbica~

a warm blanket of light

over two otters'
rollicking play.

Contours
2002

(dedicated to Peter Carter)

There unfolds an outline
of friendship:

which will never fit
upon a single page:

it is

a tenor
which

in some ways,
is nothing more than
the curves of
a dented but familiar chalice

passed in the Coliseum
from one Roman to another,

a moment's pause from
the spectacle of life:

where wine is spilled, but
the interlude is perfect:

in between the rainstorms of
each generation,

A Key to the Grove and Other Poems
~*Peter Coe Verbica*~

as stage hands warp
large sheets of tin
thunder

amidst the laughter and laurels:

a true friend lends his talent

to season
or sew
or brush
or paint
or pencil
or sing

one verse
of eternity

before collapsing
like Caruso

on stage

with the tourniquet of time
wound round his
throat:

and so we stand
on our feet

and hear the trumpets
of this morning

because you portrayed

four daughters,
as if they were
a precious quartet:

perhaps

Freedom,
Fortune,
Fascination,
and Fantasy.

You caught the petals
of their youth in midair.

and held off gravity
itself:

even the Sun seemed
to stutter

such was the suspense.

You are a friend who holds
an aperture on meaning:

so before we
drink vinegar

A Key to the Grove and Other Poems
~Peter Coe Verbica~

in the Final Act:

when all actors must
take their bow:

thank you
for helping me forget that

curtain which will fall
like a bright rain
and
bleach away
even our whispers.

Sufi in the Sandstorm
2003

Despair,

sometimes
she whirls
her arms
around
you,

and
the incense
of her breath
burns your
face

like the
desert wind.

Do you hear
the sitar of
her heart,

each note
like a coin,

bouncing
from the bed
of a beggar's
wagon

and falling
upon
stones in
the street?

A Key to the Grove and Other Poems
~Peter Coe Verbica~

Her voice
comes to you,

a seductive
sorrow,

repeating
each of your
secret wishes,

upon her lips,
a sandalwood
smile.

A child draws
from a cistern
and the water
tumbles into
a pail.

Sometimes the
chime is so
clear

that it hurts my ears.

Perhaps
only the Sufi
in the sandstorm
understands,

as he spins
and spins
and spins

into glorious
forgetfulness.

Take my prayers
to the highest
mountains of
the old country.

Here,

they are
but ashes
at the bottom
of a bowl.

A Key to the Grove and Other Poems
~Peter Coe Verbica~

© 2007 by Melissa West.

Bullets of Rain
2000

I saw you
take bullets of rain
in the chest,
hungry,
on a red mud road.

It was the last
day of the year,
and you
were singing
out the solitude
in your lungs.

A nursery rhyme:
you were that
far gone,
each wagon wheel
a carousel.

The swollen smell of
thatch, wool and whiskey
which opened up
in the rivulets.

A vest prayer book
in your jacket pocket:
The one thing
that you would
sell, but
no one would buy.

So you keep it.

A Key to the Grove and Other Poems
~Peter Coe Verbica~

You tire of standing under
the eaves of a barn,
listening to pigeons,
and start to walk again.

One thought follows
you all the way home,
like a golden dog
wearing a blue bandana.

Doves at Dawn
2003
(Dedicated to my parents.)

I can't take credit
for saying that

your very essence
comes to you
in the sixteenth mile
of a marathon:

but I have seen
darkness disappear
like a dove at dawn

spooked by my footfalls.

So,
count me in
as a believer.

I break open
the Bible of today:

like fresh fruit,
tearing away the rind
of the past.

New-born,

landing feet-first into
a cradle of hills:

I breathe in
the morning incense
of Christmas present.

A Key to the Grove and Other Poems
~Peter Coe Verbica~

and run from
the cathedral
to the country:

Unbending my knees,
I find myself
in the Heaven of here.

© 2007 by Melissa West.

A Key to the Grove and Other Poems
~Peter Coe Verbica~

120 Degrees of Separation
2004-2005
(Dedicated to Nick Berg.)

It is a harsh and simple
despair
which weighs upon me

like a rusted iron carcass.

From the shaded
window,

I see it picked at
by the bird-like
fingers of children.

They peck at the copper
wires,

and forage for the brass casings.

I am within the center
of this blistering afternoon:

In between bleary-eyed
blinks,
I turn inside my temporary room:

a pyramid of firewood
shedding its scales,

a half-liter of goat milk
within a thick glass bottle,

an oilskin coat
choking a wicker chair,

my officer's cap
upside down like
an empty dinner plate:

I am in this carnival.

At 120 degrees,

I have seen
the heat bake the
heart out this country,

leaving only its soles
half-hidden by sand,

where witches and
demons have sucked the sweetness
from the raisins

though a knothole
in the pantry door.

Some days are easier than others,
but today is one of those days

when I feel like mourning
my dead.

A Key to the Grove and Other Poems
~Peter Coe Verbica~

Bicycles
2007

Have you
ever felt

the edge of
obscurity,

though everyone
knows you:

high school hero
in your hometown:

who could forget
that great end-zone catch?

You are wedged
between the past
and present:

three decades
later:

sitting behind a
picture window:

pen, paperclips,
and actuarial table:

bicyclists
free-wheel by

your red and white sign:

a family photo
from fifteen years ago
upon your metal desk:

shields you from
self pity as
you answer the phone,

smiling.

Running Buddha
2007

Buddha sits
and Buddha sleeps:

Plump and peaceful:

Smiling eyes,
drooping ears
with fruit at his feet
and coins at his toes.

I know of a Buddha
who hides under a bridge
and a lone Buddha upon
a red dresser.

Where is the running
Buddha whose feet
fall upon the warm sand?

He is the rarer Buddha,
perhaps:

not fat at all, but
lean as a warrior:

still smiling,
peaceful,

and with a
few followers
at dawn:

snipes, seagulls and the sunrise.

A Key to the Grove and Other Poems
~Peter Coe Verbica~

Artist
2007
(in memory of Nancy Patricia Coe)

My oil paintings
are stacked
in a row
like years:

my only real family
hiding
shoulder to shoulder
on the back porch

with its terra cotta tile floor
and wooden screen door.

Outside:

a vegetable garden,
oak trees,
green lawns,

cerulean pool,
grape stake fence,
and cropped hay field

with a spotted fawn
hidden in the shadows.

I draw neighbors
like water from a well:

sometimes with
pen, sometimes

with pencil,
sometimes with charcoal.

But I am not outside
in the sun today:

with my easel
or charcoal-covered
fingertips.

It is morning
and I am lying upon
goose down,

lazy bones:

tan,

depressed
in a white
river of linens:

a Conte crayon contrast:

breathing art:

I can hear blue jays.

Natural Bridges
2005

Walk with me softly
to the water.

Let us watch
Monarchs return
like beautiful
boomerangs.

Hundreds
upon
hundreds,

they bind
the afternoon hours
with copper-colored thread,

as if bookmakers
with precious pages.

Even the sand stones
blush when they land
and the air roils

as if showered
with tangerine
champagne.

Listen:
leave Autumn.

She is like an old aunt,
who overlooks the ocean.

She's senile now
and imagines
that woodland friends
keep her company,

because her
children have stopped
calling.

(They cannot forget
Winter and being
locked in cedar closets,

no matter how many ingots
pour from the Sun.)

How sad we might
wonder,
as black and orange
wings whisper
around us.

Soft as eyelashes,
they wrap like
an invisible chain

from our heads,
to our hearts,
from our hands,
to our hips.

How fragile they appear:
 these thin stain glass
windows.

A Key to the Grove and Other Poems
~Peter Coe Verbica~

I imagine each opening
and closing as
God's winking at us.

We might as well be two
lost lovers,
finding each other's fingers
like natural bridges.

Perhaps you might
ponder a Roman
palindrome:

"in girum imus nocte et consumimur igni"

("We enter the circle at night and are
consumed by fire.")

With sly smile you could chide me,

"You take me for the butterfly's
cousin. They are the ones
who fly into the flame."

"I am a moth among the Monarchs,"
I reply.

"But what am I?"
you ask quietly.

"But what am I?"

I think:

In this place

where footprints
disappear,

and waves fall
end over end
into themselves,

I don't know if I care,

as long as you are
here with me.

A Key to the Grove and Other Poems
~Peter Coe Verbica~

© 2007 by Melissa West.

A Séance in Silver
2005

So familiar,

the fear:

it makes my
ears bleed
with anticipation,

like an Englishman
on Everest,

short of breath.

She is my
seductress,
but I blame her
for nothing:

as ageless as
a pale vampire,

distilled
and
waiting,

rising from
the séance
of a Century,

to slip
into
a silver dress:

A Key to the Grove and Other Poems
~Peter Coe Verbica~

as brief as
a bartender's
smile.

See in slow motion
the stop-gap
animation of
slender
fingers
curling
around
the neck
of Veuve Clicquot.

Whether
a crystal glass
or a jam jar,

she

sparkles
with a sorrow,

like a wealthy
widow.

I hear the
orchestra's
tonsils tuning:

a violin,
an oboe,
a bass,
a flute,

and then come the
coughs,

as jagged as jazz,

or broken
reflections
upon a wall:

a silhouette of
Plato's daydreams
lost in the cellars
of Reims.

Do you know the fire:
burning inside
a chimney's throat?

Have you watched the smoke:
wade like a demon
through the amber.

How bright are the
cherubs and cherries
dancing within the flames?

Deep within oneself:

spiritless,
infernal,
molten.

But, in the light of the morning,
angels gather:

to break each other's chains

A Key to the Grove and Other Poems
~Peter Coe Verbica~

which have enslaved
generations before them:

a Book is passed
around the circle
of a Secret Society
and read in the sunlight.

The Crypt is opened:

some are chosen
and some are
left behind

and the dead
and long forgotten
are resurrected
by the tens of millions:

We witness the Second Coming

and open our eyes to
behold a Name too
Powerful
to be spoken:

The twin sisters of
Service and Sacrifice
dance with us
over the Steps.

There is nothing to say,
but much to be done:

Kiss everyone

who wishes to be kissed.

Be alive and illuminate.

Wash one another's feet
with
champagne.

A Key to the Grove and Other Poems
~Peter Coe Verbica~

© 2007 by Melissa West.

A New Blue Suit
2009

I found myself
picking out a new blue suit
for a dead man:
I had already figured
out how he was to die.

I knew him well,
like a brother.
Flesh and blood.

(You probably have a friend like that.)
We had many meals together
and he always talked
of making it big
on one deal or another.
God, could he talk.
But, whatever reason,
nothing seemed
to gel for him.

His wife had a paramour.
His dogs were getting old.
The children were almost grown up.

He was a good guy.
People by and large seemed to like him.
And, he had gotten rid of most of his vices.
Didn't even smoke an occasional cigar.

He had stopped talking bad about people
and had this odd compassion
for bullies and misfits,
like a prairie preacher.

A Key to the Grove and Other Poems
˜Peter Coe Verbica˜

So, in despair, he
talked me into taking his life,
promising me a big pay off.

At the time, I thought that I needed it.
(I had gone through a lot of money
for reasons that I won't go into
and a job, at least for me, hadn't been that easy
to find.)

Me of all people, I thought.
What the hell do I know about such things,
except from TV or the movies.

(I had shot a wild boar
when I was young,
so I figured that would count for something.

I remembered its enormous dark figure
slumped in the rusty grass,
its labored breathing,
and its tusks covered with blood.)

My friend was one of those people
smitten by his own pity.

He had these big brown soulful eyes:
like a puppy dog.

The day I went to kill him, he told me that
he'd had a change of heart,
something about a revelation,
and climbing out of a deep well.

He talked of laying on the floor
as if crucified and made of lead.
But, he had gotten up,
aching bones and all.

For some reason,
it reminded me of someone
who'd had a stroke
and was trying to remember how to walk.

He sat out on the porch, he told me.

He talked of sun on his face
and hearing birds or some other
sentimental thing.

I was glad.
I had been sleepwalking for days
before I realized that
I had been talking to myself in the mirror.

A Key to the Grove and Other Poems
~Peter Coe Verbica~

© 2012 by Justin Doward.

Wedding Bed
2009

In a big-boned house
above a beckoning sea:

a window to the wharf
frames the grand piano,
leathered books, and a
clock's metronome melody.

Upstairs, you rest
your sleepy head softly
upon a Chinese wedding bed.

Underneath smooth silk
and intertwined wood intricacy

Waves of your hair unfold
around your radiant face,

and cascade over the pillows
like waterfalls of gold.

Our silver car is the only one
parked in a grass covered court,
hidden behind the
Wisteria and prim roses.

A weathered croquet set
leans against the gate post.

Beneath the dock,
seals bark, as if in a show.

I am naked next to you

and feel your warmth:
our long lean bodies stretch toe to toe.

From your lips
honey slips:

Your eyes open slowly,
like subtle blue stars
concealed in the day sky,

While your hands wander over
the sand of who I am.

A Diamond Ring
2009

A figure in the fog

Simple and complicated
like pi

Walking alongside
the circle of the sea

A figure in the fog
moving away from me

You head towards your
own future.

A fading note,
a finger upon a piano key:

We are no longer together:

You travel toward
Your own

Lone

Infinity.

I pick up half of a seashell.
Its shape

Reminds me of
Your sad smile.

On bended knee:

A Key to the Grove and Other Poems
~Peter Coe Verbica~

I listen to the sea
for a while.

Rain begins to strike the waves:

I watch one drop fall
into a diamond ring
and
disappear.

48
2009

Once upon a time,
a woman
who hadn't been there

lived with a man
who could do anything,

but somehow managed to do nothing

(except write some lines
upon the notebook of her forehead.)

Love left me.

She was just dog-tired,
 48,
with a long, lean face:

like a pinched penny

four children
place on the tracks.

After the train passes,
the edges become
thinner than a penknife.

I remember our life together,

as innocent in the beginning
as adolescent in gym socks.

But, later,

A Key to the Grove and Other Poems
~Peter Coe Verbica~

    it swung around on us,

    knocking us down
    to the ground.

    Like a poleax.

    A dark dirt road
    from our old neighborhood

    witches its way
    underneath the oaks.

    It's like a trickle
    of dried blood

    which once coursed
    through the white wooden gates
    of happiness

    into the heart of our house.

    You pull your hand
    from the mouth of the mailbox
    and leave the bills for me to pick up later

    on a dusty desk.

Jean-Paul
2007

I.

I had a brief encounter
with Jean-Paul Sartre
today:

after he fell
about three and
a half feet,

upon his spine.

I carefully picked him up,
the proud old man.

A bit vain
in his dusty leather jacket,

he would have none of
my apologies.

He was characteristically
absent of fear,

when I set him back
upon the shelf:

he disappeared
into a window of words

like Leonardo's face
into the Mona Lisa.

II.

He is
still the
contradictory
atheist,

who might not
believe in immortality
or his soul,

but hovers about
Europe's house
like irony's ghost.

We did not talk
about the War,
or his grandmother's garden,
or his being teased
about his name in school,
or the anguish
of the Occupation,
or North African
Socialists,
or of hell being with other people.

I deciphered crude notes
in the margin,
written with a fountain
pen in deep blue ink:

"Hold on. My mind
is breaking apart
and folding into itself."

The briefest autobiography
of a dead relative:

the rest of the stitched notebooks
had gone to an incinerator
years ago.

III.

But, perhaps I should tell you
my state of mind leading up
to our imaginary discourse:

my thoughts spooked like
a herd of jagged horses
in motion,
cantering over
a California hillside:

beautiful, jolting, lumbering:

but have none of that:

as I meander about
a shuttered Colonial:
its chimneys like horns;

briefly, I am the firefly
inside a smoking skull:

one lazy eye
dancing out to the ocean
and the other to a manicured
fairway and a white flag.

I'll surrender for now.

IV.

Beneath the Pacific,
a colossal chasm
diving deep
into the darkness:

where translucent fish
swim like phosphorous ghouls
in silence.

To most, this unseen gorge is
not given any thought.

I exonerate them.
Let them abandon their bottles
and play amidst the gulls.

I would rather take my pilgrimage
with them along the beach
and ponder the Holy Grail
under each sun dress:

that common miracle
so often forgotten:

"It is by dying that one is
awakened to
eternal life."

The oxymoron
confounds:

until an idiot savant,

jester or even Shakespeare
takes the stage:

perhaps it simply means that

the Saint and the Hedonist
have finally wed,

to spite their feuding families:

"la petit mort"
welcomes us to the
relay race:

and immortality's umbilical
is just a tenuous lifeline
between generations,

where "I" becomes "we"
and "they" become "us."

Time's reign,
like harsh droplets,
will chisel a face or two
into granite,

but I hope that
we never forget
the magnificence of
ordinary words
between a parent and a child:

this conspiracy of life.

Glorious!

V.

I nominate ashen-faced Francis
to pray for us fritterers,
while he waits patiently underneath
doves' wings and
bouquets of white magnolias.

Who can blame us?

Our addictions:
liquor and lust,
caffeine and mortgages,
expectations and jealousies,

they doom us
to agitate like
electrons.

But on good days:

For some reason,
we become in
restless harmony
with the unseen:

as if taunted by the gravity
of the moon
which pulls
on the hair of our planet
like a rough sibling.

I have been
wondering when
these tectonic arms

will break their chains
like a blind Samson in an
underground
Temple,

as we run north
while the rest
of the Continent
grinds south.

VI.

I send this to you,
tethered to a silver balloon,
just in case:

you can pick it up,
like a microwave beam
as it bounces off of the moon.

This is compounded, to be sure,
by my uneasy understanding of history:

African, Ancient American, Asian,
Arabic, Greek, Roman, Jewish, Christian,

initially Pangaea,
but ultimately breaking
into the continents of
our individual losses and triumphs,

like a treasured vase
falling upon
the floor,
the chattering pieces
awakening

the tenants below.

I salvage the moment
into mortar and make
a mosaic.

VII.

Witness the
cartwheels of youth
upon the giant spring
of science:

trouble beneath our feet:

that knot of knowledge:

a molten serpent
dwelling inside the earth,
ready to uncoil
without warning:

the basic math of
a function
running
within a function.

I remember a sepia photograph
of still horses in the street,
which leaps to my mind
from an out-of-print school book:

Their carriage overturned,

quiet and without burden,

they lay down
like fallen idols
among rubble:

hooves and limbs
dead to dance.

When I think
about their
Nothingness
after Being,
it still saddens me.

VIII.

I feel like that soldier pilgrim
who returns to the husk
of his hometown,

with just the wind,
the sprung half
of a Dutch door,
and

the bloodshot cornea
of the sun blinking
through a broken window.

Thin livestock
malinger in
the center square.

IX.

This isn't much different than other
forebodings felt by most:

they throb through a collective,
catastrophic consciousness now,
reluctant resurrections
of alternate currents:

the hands of history
break through the sod.

Whether
Easter Island's dilemma:

where only the large sculpted
heads are left to silently bray for rain,

or viruses
paint their permutations
in our blood,
waiting to jump
into humanity's panorama,

or
a forest of flashes
radiates upon the horizon,
roiling sand and stone
into molten flowers,

or a meteor smashes
into the solar plexus
of Siberia,

will we survive the promenade of suffering?

There is something insane, but heroic in this.

X.

Earlier in the day,

a red-tailed hawk
glides through the sky,

the breeze like a hand over a harp:

through the leaves of
bay, Manzanita,
acacia and oak.

I walk up
brick steps,
past a dry marble fountain
in the garden,

There are 13 stairs,
buried into the hill
like quiet apostles.

And, though I am not
a good Catholic,

they become as rote
in my memory
as the Rosary.

I enter the study like
a friar foraging for food.

At my desk,
I find myself writing letters to you.

Forgive me for not sending them.

A Key to the Grove and Other Poems
~Peter Coe Verbica~

They are a bit like prayers.

I open my fist
and take out a square of sugar.

I drop it into the white foam and watch
it disappear into a dimple.

I think about the magnet
of a moving Earth
which holds my spoon and saucer
onto the table:

it is then that I realize
that I am a touch crazy:

listening to Vivaldi's violins
and staring at a little silver Shiva:

bittersweet Turkish coffee
upon my tongue.

A Rain of Rice
2004 and 2013

"The smaller the village,
the bigger the hearts,"

Father Adriano shares with us
inside the 14th Century
church

above the Amalfi Coast's
sparkling sea.

We stand
upon a worn red tongue
of carpet,

my young wife to be and I,

black and white,

inside the cathedral's mouth.

Behind its teeth of smooth stones
and shining stain-glass eyes,

it lives and breathes,

an amber incense
of memories:

a baby's baptism,
a Papal visit,
a quiet widow's Rosary,
our wedding vows:

A Key to the Grove and Other Poems
~Peter Coe Verbica~

we might as well be
inside the belly of a whale,

ready to descend beneath
the blue-slate waves.

For a moment, I am
half-hypnotized, walking

past each pebbled prism,
upon the walls
cascades of cobalt and cranberry:

the sum of saintly sacrifices
light the center of our path.

Once through the lean pews,
we run down the steps,

underneath a rain
of rice,

as bells ring over the Moorish
houses

with the Sun itself
winking in each window.

"The smaller the village,
the bigger the families,"
I laugh,

as we climb upon the
upholstered seat
of the horse-drawn carriage,

and after the whistle
of the driver's whip,

we turn to see
wedding ribbons behind us,
waving like the arms of children
in the wind:

"Li amiano! We love you!"
we yell to
friends, family and turisti,

our hearts rising
like fresh bread in
the oven of the warm
afternoon.

Perhaps even my parents
are kissed with scent of our happiness
all the way up through
the narrow streets of Heaven.

A Key to the Grove and Other Poems
~Peter Coe Verbica~

Style
© 2007 by Peter Verbica

Black eyes of mascara
and long lashes
on pretty party girls:

Soul, serenity, and sweetness
of beliefs guarded
at the club's entrance.

They fidget
like expectant tourists,

holograms in the headlamps:

pinned to warehouse walls.

Thin as cigarettes,
I see them returning to
where they've already been:

somewhere between
angels and moths,
they are
attracted to the light.

I understand.

Bruised biceps
take away the
fairy tale's bones

and leave the early morning hours
barefoot,

high heels in hands
and feet upon the
warm and dirty cement.

A tin-foil balloon
on a string by a doorway
bounces upon my cheek

with all of the softness
of a butterfly kiss.

What am I doing here:
tuxedo observer, guest, athlete, friend.

How do you embrace
upon this square of frozen sand
where ground glass sparkles
while the rest of the word
is sleeping?

Perhaps just a match, a half-smile, and
a shaky light in hand,

at the end of a cigarette
like an orange circle
glowing in a black sky

is enough.

My guess is that happiness
won't hide behind a velvet rope…
That instead,
she loves the sun and the light of day.

I see her running through a sprinkler
as uninhibited as an eight year old.

A Key to the Grove and Other Poems
~Peter Coe Verbica~

If you close your eyes, you can hear
the wet whispers:

brass arms of a lawn sprinkler,
chopping through the water
as it cascades over a crew-cut green.

My only desire is to leave.

Christmas
2007 and 2008

It is
a beautiful curse:
being able to see
inside the bones of things:

to see the feather
inside of feathers:

to see hearts beating
underneath the shag
or shearling:

like a mystic
hypnotized by the music
of muscles:

or a grandmother
who sees her mother
in the face of a grandchild:

that perpetual clock
of God,
telling multi-dimensional time.

Who envies the deaf
requesting more miracles?

To those seeing
only a procession,
or a pantomime:

'It is already here!'
I feel like shouting,

A Key to the Grove and Other Poems
~Peter Coe Verbica~

'and the symphony
overwhelms me.'

Despite the presence
this Christmas
morning

Despite the light
splintering
through
the frozen pines

Despite boughs
outstretched
with asymmetrical offerings:

I am a still wandering,

looking for the Father:

illogically
waiting for dark trees to ignite
so that I can believe:

uncertain with
The Story's
ending or perhaps
its beginning:

two bickering twins
inside me:

a yin and yang engine.

If you share my

half-hearted
ritual:

and worry
that Truth
will bring us to our
knees:

say an Apocalypse,
rather than
ignorance's
mercy:

are we damned?

For there is nothing worse
than doubt:

dementia's despair
which freezes
like ice on Winter's windows.

Some say that
He's the
Reckoner.

(Only the blasphemes
would call Him

a Lecturer or
the King of One Night Stands:
visiting a young virgin
in the dark:

even most heretics
would blush at the impropriety.)

A Key to the Grove and Other Poems
~Peter Coe Verbica~

There are days
when I'd like more details,
call it a clinician's curiosity…

but if I'm really honest,
I'm usually
too busy to listen
and too lazy to investigate

that which balances midair
and levitates a life between
the confluence of circumstances.

The explanation, I admit,
may be beyond my
comprehension:

the combination forever changing:

the hand of the locksmith
devilishly re-tinkering with the tumblers:

A diamond with facets
mirroring facets,
maddening,
complex:

linking
Thought and Matter:

unspeakable joy and horror:
like Janus:
all at once, both the faces
of Life and Death.

But there's the young Mother
left behind:

at her feet,
straw as white
as lilies

and in her arms,
a cradled child.

That miraculous gift,
no matter what:

Motherhood.

Whether you believe
Her to be a sinner
or a saint:

a hint of forgiveness,
half-hidden,
like a statue in a niche:

perhaps it is just our
own mea culpa:
for bringing forth
children of mortals:

a new generation
sentenced to die:

the guilt overwhelms us
and
sandwiches into our
psychology.

A Key to the Grove and Other Poems
~Peter Coe Verbica~

Taken, literally,
a rape.
Taken literally,
a bastard.

Religion at its best:

a conundrum:
standing everything on its head:

making the ugly beautiful,
the poorest rich,
the weakest strong,
and the dying immortal:

we are left as confused
as Joseph and asked to trust
and accept the Nonsensical.

There is something noble
in this Divine Craziness.

A few pilgrims claim
to have heard the voice
of God himself,

as he cried out
under a northern star:

"I am alive!"
"I am hungry!"
"I need to be held!"

that raucous, beautiful sound

of a new universe
just beginning to unfold.

A Key to the Grove and Other Poems
~Peter Coe Verbica~

A Day before Christmas
2006

Forgive my
Old World
sentiments:

suspenseful,
anticipating,
desirous.

Be you a maid or a maiden or an
early morning flower afire under
April's sky: light bright
upon your skin, a radiance.

This is my burden:
your purity burns my eyes.

I am at times
too obvious
even in
a fitted tuxedo:

tall and stalwart
with a Slavic
sorrow:

a slender hand
holding a crystal
glass on polished
wood.

Whether it is
the mountains

or the mansion
or your mystery,

I watch you:
mesmerized.

Your slightest
smile

motivates marble
better than Michelangelo:

for you transform
statues into men:

perhaps it is the hint
of a warmer fire

which draws them
from the darkness
like Durer.

Dressed in red,
you drench the ballroom
in the deep colors of your
dancing flame:

your alchemy
ignites the night
and turns it into gold:

Animated
Autumn
leaves
alive,

A Key to the Grove and Other Poems
~Peter Coe Verbica~

like children
they run
in the wind.

And, your spark follows
the fuse to my heart,

which, like a brittle bone,
feels like breaking:

a brick bursting
through glass:

a bomb blowing open
French doors,

you hurl the pages
of who I am
into the public garden:

an anarchy of
emotion.

Old ideas leap
like fugitives
from a stone balustrade:

and run like
royalty.

Damn the stories:

they can stand the impact.

You sever the tether between

the animal and divine:

a mirror of motion:
you are music.

Watching you,
I discover

a rose
hidden in a lute,
carved from a single
piece of wood.

You are the instrument:
I feel notes
resonate from you:

even when you your
mouth is closed:

you levitate me
across the floor:

into your arms:
no longer a ghost.

Perhaps this is a poem
which is best left unread:

bare earth
naked without
even the loincloth of a forest:

the heart of a
monastery
exposed upon a mountain:

A Key to the Grove and Other Poems
~Peter Coe Verbica~

Crna Gora:

so much of this you have
heard before; it comes from
a choir of other lips:

they bring copper
to your gold, a carnation
to your lily,
simplicity to your mystery,
a solstice to your
resurrection,

screams to your cannons.

Discard their songs:
let us chant
like Orthodox Bishops

tone over tone

from those
melancholy hymnals
which are hidden in
your heart,

like a wayward poet
who somehow climbed
over your walls
and

wedged like
a keystone into your arch:

nave, galleries, arcades
capitals and columns,

you are
Byzantine, brilliant and beautiful.

Proud men do cry
your name:
a tear upon the tongue:

you reappear out of the fog
like a warrior princess:

your independence regained.

Whether you are
a whirlwind in red,
or a twist of verses when read:

All eyes fall upon
your enchanted dance:

a lace handkerchief
falling in the Summer
from an open window,

swung in suspense
like the seed of a dandelion,

your fleet feet
float upon
the shining floor:

my arms ache.

Your movements untie

A Key to the Grove and Other Poems
~Peter Coe Verbica~

reality's ribbon
and unwind
the sacred scroll
of what you are:

willows in the wind
upon an ever-flowing river:
alive, rustling, growing:

for you are
unconquered, yet vulnerable,
fearful, but brave;
awkward but graceful;
uncertain but steadfast;
impoverished, yet rich:

Like a mythical bird
with twin heads:

one facing Rome and
one facing Constantinople:

caught in a crimson flag
which flutters above
a parapet,

rising like a dream
from the desert:

you are the epiphany:

both the East
and the West:

where night

meets the day,
and melody meets the moment:

your inner voices
intertwine
and reveal your complexity
in their echoes:

for there is
more than one
of you:

wave upon wave from
the crowd
weave together
to become your sea
of support:

whether your
dark desperation
crashes into barriers:
or bright elation
embraces the warmest of shores:

you rise up,
like a spirit
to the sky.

So, forgive my sentiments,
when I tell
you that your golden face is
like the spring sun

which opens hearts in
a closed country:

let eternity's heavy fingers
write about my joy in
seeing your nimble flight
and your smile of white:

for I am a pilgrim soldier,
who, though battle weary,
finds renewed faith
upon your sight,

like a golden thread
of heated honey,
falling like a
string
into that
cherished bowl
of promise which
we call home.

You break me
from dim specters
of the damned and
let me rise like smoke
above the clay rooftops
to merge with the dawn.

Your hands shimmer like rivers:
as they weave through the
aura of your silken hair.

Hakone
1999

I walk on a gravel path,
bordered by cobblestones,

unevenly stacked
like peasant bread
within a wind tunnel of
wisteria.

How many trips up this hill did
the mason make,
so that this dappled terrace
could unlock the vault of my senses?

(They climb into my consciousness,
like hungry children over a locked gate.)

I am grateful to the gardener,
anonymous
under a straw hat,
who tends to each sight
and scent.

I hear the
black and yellow sound
of bumble bees buzzing
through bamboo
like fat fish.

I watch them swim through the air.

The trunks of time
have wrapped around
tall, lean-to posts like snakes,

or wooden wristwatches
which are forever wound.

If you look
long enough
at these bark-covered biceps,
you can see them
constricting
like boas.

I can't really blame them.
Who would want
to let any of this beauty go?

At my feet,
the stop motion sequence of
a small jumping spider
has me lusting for a magnifying glass.

I want to undress every aspect
of this afternoon
and kiss the soft down of its belly.

Everything that I need is here:

the quadraphonic clicks of crickets,
half-hidden maples in red flames below the Koi,
and the crosstalk of noisy Blue Jays,

which interrupt my thoughts of you.

(I remember all
that you have forgotten.

I remember unfolding
your soft hands
as if solving a puzzle.

I remember your
warm breath in my ear.

I remember too much.)

I sit on a lone bench
of wood married to wood.

I might as well be a monk in nature's train
station.

Today, I count the dragonflies and skimmers
before dozing off to sleep in the shadows.

There will be plenty of shoes
to shine tomorrow.

This moment is like
a lemon drop of sun on my tongue.

(Put your lips to my forehead.
Kiss me before I sail up through the trees.)

A Key to the Grove and Other Poems
~Peter Coe Verbica~

Paris and Milan
2001

Beautiful red petals of fame
burnt your hotel of anonymity down,

forcing you to hole up
like a fugitive in
a shuttered room
with only candles, caviar,
and grapes sweating in a bowl.

I remember you like a rose
held in gravity's teeth,
when you leapt from fourteenth floor.

Everyone closed their eyes,
expecting to find
nothing more than a still heart
on the sidewalk.

Perhaps some brave trembling hands
would discover a Czech matchbox
with a long-distance number
in your jacket pocket.

How you surprised them
when your parachute opened
to stanza 49 of a Persian poem.

Spring brings you

Confident
Nonchalant
A rhythm of graceful speed.

But your life has been like that:
a photo-finish of hooves at the finish line.

You stroll upon the runway,
in fabric as thin as your fear,

putting your finger to your lips:
our secret signal.

Who could imagine that this was only the
beginning?

You were unknown
until I named you
first after Paris and last after Milan:

These designations protect you:
like a gold sword upon a gold shield.

two cities who hate each other like sisters.

two cities who would die for each other like
brothers.

two cities who laugh and cry in one another's
arms,

remembering their saints
and forgetting their sinners.

Your Christening made you destined
to carry on a legend.

When the village priest put his hands
in a marble vase

and came up with
what the whole parish knew was only
ordinary water,

I knew that this miracle meant only one thing:

you would outlive every monument in the
street,
like the engines of green grass busy at statues'
feet.

Let champagne gracefully slip down the sides
of crystal glasses.

You know I will not drink.

But I promise
to never reveal your longing:

it is the force inside of you which gives you
wings
and a magic in the eyes of tomorrow's
children.

The Ascension
 2001 and 2013

That same voice spoke
to me this morning
with a hangman's civility:

what saints call
a hunger hallucination.

I could smell it coming like my own burning
flesh.

Lately,
everything that I am
seems to be at stake.

Each moment is kindling,
neatly stacked around my feet.

Forgive me.

I repent for writing each line
as if it was a bastard.

I know that phrases should be family.

I know that they should eat together at
the same table,

under one roof,
in a farmhouse at the end of the road.

Let me absolve myself
before a struck match combusts my soul.

A Key to the Grove and Other Poems
~Peter Coe Verbica~

This is the sincere conversation
between the chosen and the damned:
one craves the other.

Scatter the potash of my words
over fields of potatoes.

I want to help end this famine,
this starving for lyrics.

Let the smoke of what I was
put a tear in the Moon's eye.

I want to pick up what you
say like an oak leaf
and study each vein.

I want to read what you
write standing up
so that I might give hope to those laid down.

I want the dark halo
of your words to form
a circle around what is real:

like somber stain in a hatband.

I was taught to worship standing up
by a man now laying down.

"Work is a prayer,"
the man with the Stetson says.

Sickles of sweat
weep through

the sides of his western shirt.

He pays me, so
I won't argue.

I respect him because
he swallows his tobacco juice
rather than spitting it out like
the rest of us.

And, of course, he owns
the Valley:

its history had grown into
his solar plexus like
the root of a 40 foot oak,

or maybe it had become a psalm
of your choice which sleeps
forever in his skull.

If work is a prayer,
then the rhythm of it
comes to you on the last
80 acres of bales:

you load the truck without thinking:
an emotionless motion:

a conveyor wags
alongside a flatbed truck
like a loyal dog
digging in the field

with its dry metal teeth.

A Key to the Grove and Other Poems
~Peter Coe Verbica~

The bone is unearthed
and held in the muzzle:

Eureka!

It is the smell of summer.

Circling black birds
give added geometry

to the straight hewn lines down
the Valley's middle.

Sounds that the
top-heavy contraption makes,

each ratchet,
each rattle,
each squeak,

sing to you off-key
years later,

like a nostalgic relative.

I think it's on the 7 x 7 x 7th bale
that you begin to understand
the rhythm and the ritual:

you swing the hay hooks from
your sides and let them bite
into big biscuits of straw.

My grandfather repeats that "work is a
prayer,"

so I pray with hay hooks and let them
minister to alfalfa bales in the August heat.

It's when the dust gets as course
as a hobo's homily,

that I remember:

the whiskey-taste of dirt
and oat straw
the color of spun honey.

When the sun rope burns
the back of my neck
in the noose of
the afternoon,

I remember a gallon jug
of spring water
wrapped in a wet gunny sack,

 tied taut with baling twine.

The makeshift canteen
rocks back and forth
in the flatbed

like a drowsy drunk
fighting off sleep.

I unscrew the metal cap
off of the bottle's throat
and pull the glass finger-loop

towards my shoulder.

A Key to the Grove and Other Poems
~Peter Coe Verbica~

Evaporation has kept the water cool.

We take our turns chugging
in a countryside communion.

The secret is to lift the bales with your knees:
to take the strain off of the small of your back.

To get the hay through the loft's doors,
we use a pulley, rope and tractor,

and a large triangle with teeth.

We pull the line with a wheel tractor,

and sink the metal jaws,
set the spring trap
into each bale and launch them up
four stories high.

And, when a bale rises up
on twisting rope
and enters the barn doors,

and you stare into the midday sun,

silently smiling
in your own salt and stink,

it is as beautiful as
the Ascension.

To My Friends
2000

Forgive me for saying
in minutes
what I would rather write
about over years,

and bestow
with wisdom's bent back
to the children of your children,

the story of our friendship:

so that they too might
gaze out from this,
the highest window,
and view the expanse
of a magnificent bridge,

which connects us in
fellowship.

But rather than regret
the future, or nurture
wistful nostalgia,
let us unwrap the present,
around the circle
of this round table:

and say what needs to be said.

I raise a toast to celebrate
all of you,
you who do not care
what I do,

A Key to the Grove and Other Poems
~Peter Coe Verbica~

but instead care
enough to ask why.

I raise a toast to each of
you,
with this glass filled
with light,
which lacks the spirit
of the grape,
but holds a prism even more precious.

For if this chalice
rocked within its cradle
all of the wine in the world,
it could not compare
to the spirit of my
gratitude for each of you.

This simple goblet, the
marriage of fire and sand,
sparkles with our moment together
and reflects its clarity.

May it be a shining tribute
to the Marathon of
our friendship:
where the crowd at the
starting gate thins
in the open field.

Across the distant hills
of Athens,
Sinai,
Montenegro,
Kerry,

Tuscany and Tibet:

each of you have entered
into the vast stadium
of my heart,

hours before the footfalls
of other runners.

You alone come round
the longest lap,
carrying this torch
lit with friendship.

This is my standing ovation.

May my cheer for you
be the thunder,
which deafens any doubts:

for you are lightening
as you run,
full speed,
into the thin ribbon
which we call life.

Mysterious Initials
1998

I prayed
with earnest
over my mother's
grave.

I looked
into her baked
porcelain photograph
until it blurred.

I was surprised at
my sincerity.

"Please send us a
Poet, who does
not ride into town
on a Donkey.

"Save us from the
indignity of
laminated gold over
green wood
and statues of red-eyed
prophets with broken fingers.

"No one cares anymore
about the mysterious
initials at their feet.

"Most of all,
save us from our own
mediocrity.

"I am tired of smearing
burnt palm ashes
on my forehead.

"I am sick of resoled shoes.

"I would sell my body
for a box of pencils,
a pad of clean paper,
a sharp pocketknife,
and an appropriate allegory
for this generation."

I can remember my grandfather
standing in the thick powder
of our corral.

He had a tobacco-stained chin,
cracked hands, and a cotton
handkerchief around his neck.

He would de-horn the steers
and I was
the little entertainer:
cauterizing the fresh holes
with a hot blunt iron.

I remember the blood
spraying all over my
shirt and trying not to trip
over my rolled-up pants.

I remember the stench of
creosote and burning hair.

A Key to the Grove and Other Poems
~Peter Coe Verbica~

I remember
dodging rawhide
lariats and listening to
the bawling of calves.

At seven years old,
horses and houses
always seem bigger.

I went back and climbed over an
eight foot fence and stood in the
center of the circle.

I thought that I was alone until
I noticed the shadow of
a buzzard sweeping through
the field:

it sliced through my silhouette,
but foretold nothing of the
upcoming drought.

The Wet Wheel
1999

I have been playing a game of chess
with my loneliness all morning.
(We are evenly matched.)

I sit in our hidden house,
trading daydreams
for cappuccinos.

Here is my favorite:

I remember your reflection
on integrity:

black, blue, and blinking.

Every hand in my head
throws a coin into
this fountain of magnificence,

where a naked Hypatia
stands animated and immortal.

She listens patiently
to the water streaming
from each Piscean mouth.

At night,
when your eyes are
heavy with sleeping,

I wade in barefoot
just to tickle her feet
and warn her about

A Key to the Grove and Other Poems
~Peter Coe Verbica~

tomorrow's mob:

They will damn her for knowing.
My clothes wick her tears:
Her final philosophy is simple physics.

I fish for each shiny thought
of you resting under the water.

I am uncertain
what to do with so much change:
like an acolyte
with Easter's collection.

I spend an entire
morning window-shopping
for rainbows, but
worry that they are out of fashion.

I settle on a meerschaum memory:
that soft carving which turns
beautiful and brown with time.

You and I stroll
across flagstones oiled
by the passing traffic:

the five o'clock sun makes
a final pilgrimage across
the pavement:

and winds up on psychedelics.

We take a creaking elevator
up in an old hotel built on bedrock.

The car stops for a moment
before opening:

a pause so quiet that
we hear seventeen generations
of Medicis whispering their sins
to the Pope.

How high the price
of salvation
from seven stories up,

cradled in your arms,
like a baby or a bomb:

yours to jettison
or embrace.

You understand Eros:

words are the spokes
that hold the spinning.

I am what you put into
your body to stop
the shaking.

You are the asylum
for my crazed kisses.

We become a
wheel of wonder:

warm, wet, and inter-linking.

When we are apart,
I am a walking
memorial to
my own holocaust,

on the roofline
unobserved.

At noon,
snipers, pigeons, and tight-rope walkers,
window washers, sunbathers and suicidals,
gather round you like disciples.

Your gospel is simple:

"Poets make poor preachers."

I share this conviction and
apologize to the dry cleaner
for each paperback anthology.

(She pins her gossip
onto each of my starched shirts.
I become confidant and witness
to every overdue account
in the neighborhood.)

Listen.

I have seen honor
transmute
marble into gossamer
and the memory
of the dead
magically brought

to life:

each year constructs
a story upon story,

until only a building
of books remains,

where even the most
convincing speeches
from the balconies
are all but forgotten.

Most below ignore
the tower bells,
which beckon

Faithfulness
and
Passion

out from their corners:

Like two boxers,
they battle vertigo
and veritas
and dance until
there are holes in their shoes.

Bride and groom
in animus:
each heir wants the throne.

At the cathedral's
elegant promenade,
a couple winds

within a prayer path:

carefully walking
within the lines,

they will finish where
they began:

full of meditation,
and that which
empties their imagination.

Perhaps God will
forgive us for floating
over their footsteps
when they left:

I am convinced that He and She
have had enough of symbolism and rote:

at least for the last wink
of this century.

Green lawns surround
a well and hold
the birds hostage:

The police negotiator re-reads
the ransom:

"Bring history in plain paper bags.
I want to re-write it.

Undo the pyramids stone by stone:
slavery is a macabre mathematic.

Let Plato spit out his poison.
I will personally open his penitentiary.

Let Christ convince his siblings that he is sane.
He deserves this miracle.

Let Arabia and Judea concede Jerusalem.
Peace is the only real religion.

Shake Juliet until she awakes.

Let the hands of God and Adam meet on the
ceiling of the Sistine Chapel.
They have had enough of longing."

Burgundy roses aid
and abet: counting
the gold fish:

one, two and three,
rhyming into infinity.

A familiar blonde dog
investigates
the essence of humanity:

adrift like an invisible demon.

Bicyclists rest,
dead tired in the afternoon.

Meanwhile,
in front of salmon-colored sandstone,
a boy and a girl are caught
in a medieval game of catch.

A Key to the Grove and Other Poems
~Peter Coe Verbica~

You are wrapped in the sheer
curtain, looking downward
like daylight.

I remember you:

your features synthesizing
perfectly:

like DaVinci's self portrait
into the Mona Lisa.

I love you in front of a mirror:
we make a graduate study of God's icons.

Can anyone censure you for
your enigmatic smile?

Alone,
today is a day
which makes no sense:

like a boy in a blue dress

or a girl who hates perfume.

I have seen
the male and female
align themselves
like planets,

once in motion, they
remain out of each other's
reach for a lifetime.

I think too fast
and speak too slowly.

It comes to this when
I get up to leave my table:

You are the carpenter
who has taken a plane
to my door.

I am deafened by the engines.

Beyond Your Blue Eyes
1999

Beyond your blue eyes,
we twist our tongues together:
a naked brunch under a moist sky.

Each minute is like a pearl from a
pomegranate:
I bite the juice gently from your lips:

We mimic the waves,
which we catch naked in a rhythm on the sand.

I long for your taste of sweet and sour,
like powdered sugar on lemons,
like honey twirling down from a salty spoon.

Pull me slowly into you and
whisper every secret wish:

we are like turbinado crystals,
which dissolve into a black and silver mirror --
gone forever,
a brushstroke.

Spend every morning,
Spend every afternoon,
Spend every evening with me in this linen bed:

Feel the gentle gears of the universe,
and press yourself against me once more.

Oak transforms into embers on our patio.
Intertwined,

we watch the miracle with sleepy eyes.

The smoky spirit of the wood ascends in a column
over the Mission's tiled roof.

It rises above the palms as if to read their
fortune.

And when our fire traces a line in the sky,
it becomes a string anchored to an invisible
kite.

We witness the transcendence, as if for the first
time.

Then, the cool shade reminds me that I am
here with you.

How still I become underneath these trees.

It is the forest of men that women burn down
with summer lightening.

This heartbreak is the dust upon my feet which
keeps me from flying into the
sky.

You kiss me like Judas in front of the open
blind. How beautiful you are in
your betrayal.

I listen to near and far sounds:

thick china on top of Portuguese tiles in the
kitchen downstairs,

a neighbor hitting a tennis ball
against the side of a stucco garage,

a distant cigarette boat in full throttle on the
Bay.

You begin to count the shades of green in the
trees,
but run out of numbers.

Unbutton your shirt again and let me confess
to each obsession in a language
that you may never fully understand.

Piano Climbing
1999

The mountain which is
within me met your music:

my fingers are
numb from pounding these
keys:

like a mountain climber's
frost-bitten claws around
a carabineer:

slowing letting out the rope
of each note...

Rappelling down,
scaling,
the path becomes
dangerous

-- almost absent of melody.

I leave behind the
very ground
which I love,

and hang
from the sheer cliff
of music:

just to taste you.

(I remember breathing air too thin
for the blades of helicopters.

A Key to the Grove and Other Poems
~Peter Coe Verbica~

It is was that lonesome
and did not make me
stronger.)

I begin to hear
voices melt into the rhythm:

"Forget the timing
and the cleats on your feet.
Become the chorus
in the heart of this mountain."

Your memory
transcends the scene
and season:

like steam from an iron
coffee pot.

(My antenna receives your strong signal.
I am excited by your voice.)

I look into ice,

airborne,
crystalline,
diamonds:

grinding into
graphite.

On top of the world,
hallucinations wrap around
me like prayer flags:

I watch oxygen undress into ozone.

Ten days later,
safe and grounded:
on the other side
of the world.

The piano's belly
rumbles in hunger:

a metronome
drowning out
a sorrow
within the sea.

I look
outside the
French doors.

Right now,
I wish that the water
would just pour into
the windows.

I am that overwhelmed
by a duet which sits silent
in front of me.

What good are two arms
when four are needed?

I know how Shiva feels
when he must dance without a disciple.

If the wind were to

pirouette an apparition
in the sand,
this evening, I would not notice.

I am that somber.

Every word is foreclosed
and each paragraph shuttered.
My phrases march, slip and stutter.

It is the off season.
I play to phantom strings.
I perform for my ghosts.

Behold the opening to nature's ballet.

Raise a glass to this pianist.
These hours of sadness
have made me mad:

I stare at
a stem which has
drawn the water from the vase
and yearn for your flower.

(You anticipated me
anticipating you:

and warned me not to lose
myself in
mirrors reflecting mirrors.

I found myself suspended
in that chasm of
infinite possibilities.

"What are images without
a story," you asked.)

All I have become is the notes.

Tonight,
there is nothing left of me.

I am the axis of the world.
A heart of longing.
A rusted door at the foot of Tibet.

Tennis
2008

When you hit,

it's like the
crushing of a grape

that sweet
and
that bitter,

an addiction
that takes you
beyond love:

tennis.

The Perfect Place
1999

This is the perfect place
to be lonely for you,
on a redwood deck
overlooking the ocean.

I chose the best view in the hotel,
so that your memory
would have a balcony from which to jump
like a baby into open arms.

No one knows that I am here,
and yet I find myself wondering why
there are no messages.

I will tell you that the beach is beautiful,
but the water is very cold:

It took an hour to massage
the chill out of my bones.

Do you remember my bad habit of
swimming out too far?

Exhausted on the sand,
I listen to my panting breath and
think of a hand-painted sign painted on a van
which I passed on the highway earlier:

It read, "DOGMAN."

The owner's despair frightened me,
because it could have become my own:

where night becomes so dark that you
can no longer see your fingers.

You will laugh if I told you
that at 4:30 this afternoon,
I poured water for you into a champagne flute:

"To clarity, to time, to reverence."
(I had no idea what I was talking about.)

Raising the glass to the horizon, it
turned the trees and sky upside down.

A clear, brilliant hyperbole at dusk:
a strange magnifier, like a writer's mind.

I would like to have introduced you to my
three friends:
we dined on fresh toast and the sweetest
butter.

They were dressed in black,
but they were not somber.
(I think that you would have enjoyed their
noisy company.)
One had a broken foot,
and I could not keep myself from staring
(though he didn't seem to mind).
The waiter had better manners than I
and pretended not to notice.
I admired my friend's finesse as he hopped
up and down the planks.

But,

a crow doesn't worry much about
appreciation,
when he is enjoying
a thick crust of bread
on a balcony overlooking a blue ocean.

He is like a poet in residence:
feasting before the famine.

The Table
1999

I have come to kneel down at
the broken table of my ancestors:

to replace old iron with new steel,
to stable the unsure legs,
and strip off the veils of varnish,
and sand down the scars
into bright brown ashes of certainty.

(Forgive me for devaluing an antique
with practicality:
I bought this permit
and paid for the liberty by surviving.)

I have come to smell the teak as if it
were a cut flower.

I will toast everyone who has dined here
before
me: whether brilliant or bad, whether silent or
blaring,
whether meek or mumbling,
whether beautiful or dying.

Whimsical, I carve a clue underneath a leaf
for a child who will arrive like Moses in a
basket
to a mother in the future:
the messages reads, "You belong," and it is in
Braille.

I pour oil slowly from a silver can and it quenches
the thirst of a million microscopic mouths.
The wood soaks up the pool: a gathering of amber
tears, drawn from the dirt,
disappears.

For a moment, the morning glistens:
refined under a red rag and my ragged
knuckles.

I set out a clear crystal chalice and watch a robin
consecrate the water.

Without any reason whatsoever,
I begin to quietly cry.

Perhaps I am overwhelmed by the ghosts
who will be joining me later for dinner.

A Key to the Grove and Other Poems
~Peter Coe Verbica~

Conversations of Touch
1999

I was surprised to discover
my favorite book underneath
your pillow:

the one with
the solemn blue face
on its cover,

open to the chapter about
Paris and the ending
of another sad war.

(I re-read the scene
with the three characters
who did a slow waltz
together on an empty
ballroom floor.)

I began to remember:
the light across the dark planks,
that Mercator projection
stretching the world
away from the Equator.

You threw out the symbols
and substituted the sounds:
the language was new
and simpler and sweet.

I began to remember the
the Summer
afternoons in conversations

of touch:

A finger on the mouth
and the subject
often abreast of
soft and hard hidden spaces.

One long refrain
between your
thighs and between your lips:

Circuitous
tantalizing
and
verbs which shook
understanding
from the trees:

like an earthquake
rolling under ripe fruit.

The exclamations
which punctuated
each interjection

and pauses between
the sentences:

that balance of
narrative
suspended
over an abyss
of pleasure, like a royal balloon.

The unpopular places
are the best:

A Key to the Grove and Other Poems
~Peter Coe Verbica~

they hold the forgotten
secrets.

I am the prayer wheel
and you are its center.

Our tongues
like commas,
dig into
each beautiful page:

with the final chapter
unwritten
and the public
knocking on
our door.

I slip our diary to a
penitent in a cloistered order,

to one who has
peered through pane
until there was no window,
no reflection, and no rain:

Bestow this gift
to the one who prays
for the roses
and not for the bones underneath.

Whether you find our offering
in the bowl of this Millennium
or the next:

You need not

turn it over and over,
like a cube with seven sides.

For, the conversation is simple:
it is one of touch.

Leave the museum and
kiss the docent on the lips.

Feel the elation of your life.

(Slow down light
Until you can walk inside it.)

A Key to the Grove and Other Poems
~Peter Coe Verbica~

Horses in Motion
1999

I didn't believe
until I watched
man-made meteors
set the horses in motion.

The words were
under the thunder in
the ground,
hissing like fissures.

I spoke them too:

with running feet
under dark diving birds
of destruction.

It is the beautiful rain at
the beginning which
will wash away your house
with revenge
and make you pay
for sins of omission.

Bring blankets to
mysterious children,
at the mouth of
a crying cave:

They are your desires.
Protect them from the cold.

I could tell you that their hair

flies through you
and engulfs your bones,
but you know better.

My first death came
at me when you left:

I fell asleep in sadness,
in a silver craft
under the silence of the sky.

That drifting sorrow
spilled into me,
and gained velocity:

like a river of earth,
that avalanche of love in despair.

It is like a sirocco through
spinning blades that puts
an army into the air.

We foretold of our resurrection
when we left the
safety
of self-preservation:
we stopped grinding meal from
the very kernels of our fears.

There are no longer reapers where
we are going:

only wheat,
wind and wild horses.

(These are the

hours upon hours of honesty.
The birds sort out
hors d' oeuvres
on the plates of this acetic lake.)

We feed on the horizon
and wait for the plane to land,
holding hands as if in a painting.

These are the hours that
I would rather kiss your lips
than your soul.

This is the moving picture of our lives
which needs a new ending.

Where a man and a woman end
their private war,
and embrace.

Parachute
1999

My bare feet strike
at the shore,
beating back
the fear of death
with each long stride.

I am running:
when the adrenaline hits me
like the anguish of an angel.

Come with me.

We have wings
and.
little use
for clothes.

Leave
behind the
derivatives and elope:

Understand that the sun is a star.

Pull out the cord
and parachute
from your window:

you know that
I will catch you.

Leave behind
those black tar visions
and shadows on the wall.

A Key to the Grove and Other Poems
~Peter Coe Verbica~

You will find the real trees,
not just the streets
that hold their names
on green and white frames.

Pull the needle from your vein.
The liquid of this life is clearer.

Follow the shoreline until you
realize that it circles back upon itself.

There are no hostages
picking up cans here.

Throw your
bouquet of regret
from the balcony
and unknot the dread from your hair.

Open the afternoon like a papaya.

Put life's lips
to your ear:

(It is the whisper
of tranquility.)

(It is the prism
in a tear.)

(It is my chest
imploding
in your arms.)

These are the musicians
which you must meet.

You are that effortless
miracle borne from
generations of practice.

When others bang
drums and cymbals,
take the time
to listen for the flute:

it will take you above the stage.

Breaking Windows
2000

Wearing white coats,
they will be quieting me soon.

It is my turn to die.

The clock reads 6:30 above
my head:

the two hands
like scissors
in a pie over my bed.

I have watched
weird angels
walking within water:

they come
to medicate my mind
for the final unwind.

Let them settle the old trauma
with one final micro-blow to my head:

the thinnest of needles
until the emotions of me
are bleached off of the paper.

Catch a small silver key:

it falls off of my tongue
like a tear on a table.

(I know it isn't much, but unlock your
handcuffs and run like hell.)

I will French kiss this
conspiracy theorist
on her mouth:

until the hate leaves her eyes.

For she has had
the kindness
to let me spit out
my terra cotta teeth:

the loosened ivory
of my leprosy
has dropped
into the galvanized bucket
of the 20th Century:

one by one.

Perhaps you have
smelled the spice-piles of
of brown powder,
walking barefoot through
the bazaars:

it is our DNA and the nature
of transgression
which we slice like a lemon
for our tea.

These are words
which grow inside
my skull like a cyst.

I have walked the halls of
the Infinite Corridor
and held hands
with a mad mathematician.

He showed me
the formula for doom.
I understood why it was too much for him.

I have put my face up
to the rivets and the seam,
until they merged into
a hallucination
of rivulets and steam.

I have become so tired lately:
extra holes in the
topography of what was I:

they have been taking aerials
of my mind,
and mapping that
forbidden forest:

the horror of what I am
and what I am not.

Give me a month to cough
up the phlegm next to my bed:

until I am completely transfused.

They say that Satan breaks windows
in the darkness,

so that God can fix them during
the day.

"Born to die" on a bumper sticker:
trying to suck hope out of you
through your nose.

Have we come this far
to hate heroines and heroes?

Must we poison the good
and sit it in a chair,
so that we can comb hour after hour
and weave a necklace with
the loose hair?

Measure this madness,
let it eat the Orient
until asleep in the dark
at the end of a black
lacquered table:

thoroughly modern
and beating without a heart.

I waved goodbye to the Renaissance.
I waved goodbye to the pain.

I have watched my entire
family burn to death
in the rain.

Colors of Koi
2002

How quietly the colors of Koi
slide below
the water's surface.

Who but the gardener
knows the turtle
which snaps at them?

In the Morning
2002

Our teak Pagoda
hides in an archipelago
of cherry blossoms.

I sip black tea
and watch steam
rise like spirits from the trees.

How strange to be
haunted
by each intricate
strand of a memory.

But,
who can forget
the strong smell of cinnamon
or a silk pillow
on a bed of stone?

A Key to the Grove and Other Poems
~Peter Coe Verbica~

A Spider in the Sun
2001

There is a spider
in the sun
this morning
and she spins
her amber honey
under the eaves.

Your eyes open
and share the suspense.

Sandals on My Feet
2001

Unveil your peaceful face
in this village of hate.

I will block
every thrown stone
with pages from a
forgotten poem.

I will lift you on my shoulders
and walk through ignorance
with nothing more

than sandals on my feet.

A Key to the Grove and Other Poems
~Peter Coe Verbica~

Ghosts in the Cold
2001

This evening
is like a
stairwell of blue stones

which
threaten to
take me to heaven.

It's hard for anyone
to truly understand
without smelling
a muzzle's incense.

By the time
you see the flash,
it's too late to grab
the handrail.

Even your breath
creates ghosts
in the cold.

© 2007 by Melissa West.

Gone
2001

One
drop
from an air conditioner
lands upon my forehead

and anoints me
in the heat.

There are no dogs barking
in the streets.

They have been eaten
into silence.

Pretty Songs
2001

We hold hands
and wade into the sunshine
as if it was a river
of gold.

You tempt me
to leave this land
of salt and sand and smoke
with a simple smile.

I can't blame you.

Perhaps I have become
too fascinated
watching the tongues
of children
burst into flames
while singing pretty songs of hate.

A Key to the Grove and Other Poems
~Peter Coe Verbica~

The Bridge
2002 and 2009

Michelangelo:

come down
from the
scaffold
and give
your eyes
a rest
from the ceiling:

you have been
alone too
long with
your obsession.

Come,
eat crackers
with the
Cardinal,

while I tell
you a story
which will occur
hundreds of
years after
your death.

Like you,

I have seen
the hands
of Adam

and God

take shape
within my lifetime:

their fingers
outstretch,

but still
do not touch:

outside the gates,
pigeons make
ambulatory patterns
upon courtyard stones.

If you insist to look
once again
towards the sky:

look through the
ceiling itself

to an expanding cathedral
where one
watches

new works of wonder,
which

are launched
into
in a synchronous
ballet:

each

pirouette's
spectacular
ascension

as loud as
the trumpets
of God.

I have seen
the
gallery awestruck,
like a man knocked from
a horse,

and
made
a believer.

These satellites soar
to where sounds are silent

and the old rules
of physics
unbind:

to orbit
in that
hallowed
hollow of space:

like black priests
waltzing
in a white winter.

They

return with
precision,

when their fires
darken,

prodigals in decent:

yet, nonetheless
welcomed with open arms,

as if they were angels,

by weeping fathers
and laughing mothers.

I have seen
the present
unfold
as if a flower

with foils
to capture
the energy

of roiling stars:

and mirror in
miniature
Heaven
and Earth's oscillations.

I have seen
all of this built
upon brick after brick
of failure

A Key to the Grove and Other Poems
~Peter Coe Verbica~

to form a golden bridge

which learned
to heal and
communicate with itself:

for we have all
listened to the petitions

at the wailing wall
of ignorance:

each mathematician's
algorithm

becomes an
aping permutation
of the same
prayer

sung from separate spires:

"Simplify the solution."

So we seek to
hold the elusive
and ever-changing:

like so many
glass beads
falling from a string:

umbilical signals
which bounce

and scatter
upon the ground.

We fight
our inelegant disappointments
with creativity and redundancy,
with truth and dogma,
with understanding and doubt,
with freedom and promise:

cynics would say that
these are just the snakes
which eat at their own tails.

Perhaps we should
find profound meaning

within the sheer
enormity of randomness and rule:

twin sisters in an unending debate,

their spectacular arguments
unleashing
nebulas and galaxies.

Years ago,
this was all foretold in your fresco
by sad saints with peeling faces.

God bless the monks
who, after fasting for days,
see into the
polychromatic smoke,

and resurrect

A Key to the Grove and Other Poems
~Peter Coe Verbica~

the Holy Spirit,

Which breathes meaning
into the meaningless,

a Divine
syncopation
in a sea of solar wind.

I will be
the first to admit

that all of this
seems nonsensical,

especially to
a woman
rapt in white light,

miles away.

We stand
next to
a choreographed conch
and our coffee cups,

and survey
blue domes in the dawn
like orchard owners.

Our tan arms slide
into a figure eight.

Above you,
I spy a silver satellite,

before
closing my eyes

and smelling
the sweet strawberry
of your hair.

Easter Riddles
2003

The day was as clear
as a nun's conscience.

I was eating
toasted cereal
under a Moai
on Easter Island.

Some Chileans
had pushed the
toppled statue
back up,

with the same
unthinking good
intention that

you
might chase
after a student
who had dropped
a book from a backpack.

It was the
fourth week
of April

when the sadness
submerged me
like a wall of water.

I was swept dumb

and set my
bowl down in the
rusty-green grass.

The spoon inside it
rattled briefly and then
settled in the cradle
like a brittle baby.

Perhaps it was the
silence of the monuments,

built year after year
by islanders
driven mad with famine.

I had a vision of
them begging each stone face:

"Make it rain,"

until the last tree
vanished

and the final cannibal
leapt from a cliff and
drowned in the sea
of the past's unconsciousness.

I realized that this island, like death,
only evokes the most desperate riddles.

Perhaps the kernel
of Christianity
is no different,

taunting each generation
with its questions:

who but a few understand
the real purpose of religion?

I descend into nonsensical
daydream and remember
old verses

while the wind whittles at me
with rough kisses:

Why would a father
abandon his good son
who is about to be put to death?

      "My God, my God, why have you
forsaken me?"

The resurrected live.

The ultimate penalty of nonconformity is
death.

Absolute courage and complete stupidity share
the same mother.

We assassinate honesty at every opportunity.

How often do we passively stand by while
someone in our midst is being persecuted?

Why would you trust

your kingdom to a liar?

    "Woman, I know him not."

A contrite disciple is better than a proud one.

Courage takes time.

Others often know us better than we know ourselves.

Why does a husband rejoice
when his wife is pregnant
with a child who is not his?

"But while he thought on these things,
behold, the angel of the Lord appeared unto him
in a dream, saying, Joseph, thou son of David,
fear not to take unto thee Mary thy wife:
for that which is conceived in her is of the Holy Ghost."

A child fathered by God is cherished, not despised.

Learn not to despise things merely because they are not yours.

The rich capitalize on what most would abandon.

How do you rule a Nation when defeated?

"And Pilate wrote a title, and put it on the cross.

A Key to the Grove and Other Poems
~Peter Coe Verbica~

And the writing was,
JESUS OF NAZARETH
THE KING OF THE JEWS."

A true ruler serves, rather than being served.

Be more concerned with your legacy than your life.

The ignorant destroy what is precious.

It is then that I realized,
seated at the crater's center,

here on this island surrounded
by warm water,

that my life is not about better answers.

My life is about better questions,

though on a day like today,
I want to just stay still and smell the ocean.

Gateway to a Dream
2003

Above a lone
lighthouse

as pale as
teacher's chalk,

above the
salt-spray and shoreline

and the
blackboard expanse
of the sea,

above the
washing waves,

which rise like
youthful arms
eager to answer

each of life's riddles:

I wander
though a friend's
private garden:

and it teaches me.

It is a father's tribute
to beauty
and innocence
which left us too soon:

those footsteps down
the stair-steps
of perception
into the
gateway of a dream.

I keep mostly quiet:

and pocket my words
like sand dollars

picked up along the
beach in the morning.

I pass through

an abandoned door
which frames
a shaded path

and walk
like a mute disciple:

for it is as if
I have sailed into
this decade on
a black ship

and come upon
King Minos himself,

weary of sacrifice,

lying face down in the leaves.

If only a song bird
savior,

like Ariadne,

could sing a secret into my ear:

and unwind
water
instead
of wool string
behind us as we travel

to solve
the maze of the world.

If only we could retrace our
steps to the very beginning:

before the mortar had
set between each stone

and listen to
the mouth of the ocean
as if it were our
only oracle.

Compassion is that thin
and silvery twine

which weeps
around
in the sanctuary of
this emerald arbor

and seeps

A Key to the Grove and Other Poems
~Peter Coe Verbica~

deep into
the very pebbles
of who we are.

The fountain's stream
goes underground
and repeats
this course:

a spiral within a spiral
between
heaven and earth:

a path for parents
to follow their children.

The rains fall
heaviest in the Winter.

But, for now:

the scent of Gardenias
cascades over me

and
beckons like a
whitewashed memory.

And, when
the Sun
slips down

as if an
enchanted sword
in through the palm fronds:

it slays
that horned half-beast
of sadness

which
breathes heavily in the center
of myself.

It is then that I can hear
clearly:

the airborne laughter
of a daughter
in a swing
nearby:

appreciation overwhelms me

and I share the joy
with a wave to my wife
at the window.

One Word
2003

If you could change
one word in
the poem of your life.

Which would you choose?

An Honest Afternoon
2004

My dictionary, thesaurus
and portable encyclopedia
are gone.

(I'm like a naked man on the beach in the off
season.)

The pocket books are up in my office,
but it's cold and late,

and I'm too lazy
to go outside and walk up
to the little wooden building
up our graveled drive way.

It sits like a quiet smoking Indian,
just before our brick pillars and white
wooden gates.

Under its eaves,
books are stacked,
guarded by the sentry of a pot-bellied
stove, which sits like a happy Buddha
warming one of the windows.

My thoughts are as flat, gray and pock-marked
as the courtyard outside our front door.

I live in the original clubhouse
of a golf course built in the 1920's.

It's a ghost of a Monterey Colonial amidst old
oaks,

A Key to the Grove and Other Poems
~Peter Coe Verbica~

surrounded by this evening's fog.

At dawn, our three Australian Shepherds run out
onto the putting green and provoke
the duffers, while our black cat takes refuge on the roof.

Green or red striped range balls land on the lawn
and woods in my backyard.

One of my best friends just had a stroke.
It knocked him down like an anvil.

We were oddly-linked.

Separated by 30 years,
we both wore felt cowboy hats
in this hatless harbor town.

We had also put the plug in
the jug many years back.

I'd like to think that
we were cursed with a gift
for divining absurdity

and encouraging it
in everyday conversations.

We would have coffee with friends
every Saturday at the worst restaurant in town.

After he got sick,

I would go to visit him
at the rehabilitation
center.

We would fantasize about integrating
hookers in with the nurses,

so patients could have what they really
wanted.

I leaned and listened, next to his bed.

They had him confined in a fish-mesh cube:

even in convalescence,
he understood the comedy.

We spoke of

World War II trainers
with odd numbers,

conspiracy theories,
poker games
and cruise ships,

the well-intentioned
and the chosen,
or just drunks who had died,

of prototypical places,
white-washed wards,
and unbelievable sameness,

of fiction becoming fact
and

A Key to the Grove and Other Poems
~Peter Coe Verbica~

of simple yearning,

inventions, and
the need for inelegant criticism
and the tawdriness of life,

of danger,
and domesticity.

I tried to share my sense of grief
with my wife:

she looked at me as if I was a lost
child and said nothing.

Grief did not pay for private tuitions
or ballet lessons.

Grief did not pay for tennis clubs
or dresses or mortgages.

Grief would not raise four girls and
get them married.

Her mother had died when she was
in her teens and it had put a steel
door around parts of her heart.

(I couldn't blame her.)

I helped my friend out of his gray
T-shirt and we put on a new one,
which I had purchased for him
on 41st Avenue.

It said, "Thou Shalt Not Snivel."

And, when he asked where his
watch was, I'll never forget the
joy of placing mine around his wrist.

He held its luminous dial up
and grinned as boyishly
as a Boy Scout.

We chuckled about having the
damnedest time getting a milkshake
from the hospital's kitchen.

"You know what they do to the honest
ones," I asked my friend.

"They shoot them," he answered.

"Nail them to a cross," I replied, nodding
my head slowly. "Nail them to a cross."

"I'm not sick," he said, looking at me with
one good eye.

"I'm a cripple. Call things what they are."

"I will," I answered. "I will."

The Hat Miracle
2005

"Fall on your knees.
O, hear the angel voices…"
the old entreaty
plays on
the lobby desk's
radio.

Today, I am
convinced of at
least half of it.

It is all that
I can do to
keep my canter.

A silver star
ornament
is taped on
top of the
radio's telescopic antenna:

a touch of humor
or subtle defiance.

The music
drifts into
my consciousness
like a desert
caravan,
stenciled upon
the horizon.

*I think of heavy
footfalls and
imagine
sand blowing
over dune crests:*

God's very breath.

Among the
white uniforms of
nurses
and orderlies,
I am suddenly
embarrassed to be
wearing black.

Perhaps I have been
to too many funerals.

It is the price
of living so long:

the last dark rose
in Winter's
garden.

Folding behind me,
the double fire doors
swing the
Christmas carol
into silence.

The linoleum tiles
feel sticky
under my Oxfords.

I can smell

A Key to the Grove and Other Poems
~Peter Coe Verbica~

the dying while I walk
down the wide hall.

Somehow, the odor strikes
me as out of place:

in contrast of
crayon-covered
posters,
the blinking lights,
tinsel, and
voices of children.

How strange,
 the desire
to jump straight
through a window,
but I notice
the embedded lace
of wire mesh.

I enter Room 112-A
and see
my Granddaughter
wedged in
a manger of
stuffed bears.

I place my hand on
her forehead forever
and then sit.

 "I pray
for a miracle,
Granddaddy"

the thin ten-year old says.

I barely recognize her,
but she recognizes
me.

I hear the first harmonic
of her voice and then
the overtones:

like gold glitter
falling from
a red envelope.

Her hospital overlooks
the ocean.

The edifice forms
an alabaster block,
framed by
black water,
which rolls
under a
rust-colored
bridge.

The timber of a
fog horn's long moan
oscillates in the
distance.

"What have I done wrong?"
she asks,
distracting me from
the panorama.

A Key to the Grove and Other Poems
~Peter Coe Verbica~

I listen to her,
too stupid or too
smart to answer.

Quiet at the edge
of her bed,
I am self-conscious:

willing everything,

the chairs,
the mechanical bed,
the flowers and vases,
the food tray and chocolate
milk carton,
the IV,
the heart monitor, and
the building itself

into weightlessness.

"The doctor gives me poison.
It makes me lose my hair,"
she states matter-of-factly.

I nod my head.

"Mommy brought
me a purple hat today," she says,
patting her crown.

"It's soft."

"Your Grandmummy's favorite color,"
I offer with a smile.

She smiles back.

*I am glad that my wife
died before having to see this.*

I would not wish it upon anyone.

"I miss Grandmummy,"
she whispers.

"So do I, my little angel. So do I."

"She would have wanted you to have this,"
I tell her,
pulling a silver chain
with a diamond teardrop
from my pocket,

like Drosselmeyer.

"Granddaddy, I'm worried
that I will lose it,"
she says excitedly,
holding it inside
her palm
as if it were a cricket.

"Precious things are never lost,"
I tell her.

"They are always
tucked away in
the photo album
of our heart,"
I instruct in a low tone

A Key to the Grove and Other Poems
~Peter Coe Verbica~

and place my right
hand on
my chest,
as if ready
to take a vow.

*I remember running
along the frozen river in
Colorado
years ago
in the ruddy dirt.*

*Every tree looked
the same,
like
weathered
wicker giants.*

*The coyotes were as
big as wolves,
and would cross
the trail in front of you.*

*You could hear their
feet in the leaves
as they loped by.*

*When the dry dusk came,
it grew colder and
colder.*

*All that I had for reference
was the time.*

*It allowed me
to circle back to where I was*

before nightfall.

Now, I am without bearing.

*Despair makes for poor
reverie.*

"Can you eat a milkshake?"
I ask.

"Maybe tomorrow,
Granddaddy,
when I'm not feeling sick.

Maybe Grandmummy,"
she says sleepily,
"will make me one
with whip cream."

"And, put a cherry on
the top," I add,
watching her close her eyes.

Magnificent Sadness
2006

That magnificent sadness:

I have calculated it
over and over
in slow motion

while galloping along the shore:

Muffled hooves chop
into damp sand like
Chinese chisels

and at each impact
the horse exhales
in heavy rhythm.

The foam
upon a dark sea
looks like a sweep of sweat

or perhaps a shard of sugar:
among white dunes dusted with
brine.

Bridle and bit:
Blue sky upon
black and blue water:

Moving in unison:
the rise
and fall: a sum of motion under a curve.

And the trees upon the cliffs
bend their backs without breaking.

They shrug their
shoulders and borrow from the wind.

And the airstream
mimics voices of the Apocalypse,
as if to foreshadow:

When a giant becomes
a beggar under a bridge:

When the teeth of gears rust shut
and a flag gathers dust on the moon:

Will you ride ahead to warn the
parade of the damned:

the storm is coming,
like a great wave over quiet water.

A Key to the Grove and Other Poems
~Peter Coe Verbica~

A Brief Ode to Crossfit
2006

Let me write plain veracity for once,
as unvarnished as a 2 x 4
pulled from a back bin:

because most would not believe
what we do each morning.

It would sound senseless and made up,

like a bite from a bad apple:

Who would seek the
sooty smell of diesel,

or food-scrap perfume
which haunts the air like
a tormented ghost?

What sane person would move
like iron towards a magnetized Mecca:

attracted to
smoldering coffee beans,

which burn unseen in
the heart-shaped ashtray
of the warehouse district.

Who would lust to hear
the clack-on-the-track
sound of steel roll-up doors,

just to see a cold light, like
dragon's breath from a cave,
spill upon the cement.

We climb ropes until our ankles are
as raw as cold slaw;

do pull ups until our hands bleed
beneath broken calluses;

row until we are beyond breathing,

and swing kettle bells
until our arms feel as if they
will rip out of their sockets.

We squat with barbells and
do dead lifts with dumbbells.

We still wonder how much we can do
until we drop
and then we end up doing more:

Because we are slightly insane.

We are like prisoners
who have made friends with our guards:

they leave their wooly common sense
and join us in the threadbare madness:

but we remain in the cage even though
the door is open.

It is the strangest of addictions.

A Key to the Grove and Other Poems
~Peter Coe Verbica~

We form an Indian Run and pass a
medicine ball down the line:

to return like grimacing devils
to face down a frightened clock:

Our maxim is simple:

if you're not run over by the
tractor-trailer trucks,

you get to live in glory,

until your name is erased from the board.

Peace of Immortality
2007

I found a peace of immortality
doing what I love

a door through the dying business

like a child looking at
self reflections

on a triptych dressing top mirror

that small cathedral into
oneselves.

A Key to the Grove and Other Poems
~Peter Coe Verbica~

Simple Sunlight
2009

Here are my seven sins,

like silver coins
dropped upon
a velvet-lined
offering plate.

Take them from me,
one by one.

(They are all that I have
to offer right now.)

Your words
work like water,

and weep through
through
locked doors.

They tumble
over stone walls,

and bleed into the
pages of every hymnal.

You arrive as
simple as sunlight

and free a
blue and crimson saint

trapped in a
stain glass window.

Some call you loving.
Some curse you as cruel.

Some call you personal.
Some call you dual.

To some you a three.
To some you are none.

If I am part of you,
then praying to thee,
I am praying for me.

What would you
have me do now
that I have lost
my wedding ring?

Next to the base
of a palm tree,

I listen to a lawn mower,
and open my eyes.

Can you feel the
warm breath of the afternoon,
and smell the ivory jasmine?

A cloud catches
a cross on the roof
and then releases it

into a generous sky.

A Key to the Grove and Other Poems
˜*Peter Coe Verbica*˜

Roses bloom
over buried Indians.

An adobe wall slouches
imperceptibly
under the weight of vines.

This Town
2012

My four daughters
were born here,
so I owe this town big-time.

They're off and running:
in the cross-country race of life:

but their first dream,
their first breath,
and their first teardrop

landed here:

like a raindrop upon an acorn.

And, if their eyes opened here for
the first time,

perhaps I, too, should take a
fresh look at this town:

and plant my feet firmly
into the ground and lean
forward

with everything that I am:

to wrestle those
dark angels of sorrow and cynicism

A Key to the Grove and Other Poems
~Peter Coe Verbica~

into the light:

until they tap out on the mat
out-matched

by wisdom and serenity.

I owe this town that much:

so I take a long-distance run
past Forbes Mill and Vasona,

up Saint Joseph's Hill
and down the face of the dam

and hug the spillway
like a long-lost prodigal.

It's not much of a tribute,
I admit on my cool-down
on the overpass.

But a cup of coffee
at the Roasting Company
tastes so much better

when you've earned it:

I can almost hear the
railroad whistle stop

and see the parasols:

and loggers with a fortified
glass of red wine:

grinning like Novitiates
after a good harvest.

There's a future here too,
as well as a past,
I imagine:

Someday, I'll lift my
grandchildren

into a horse-drawn
Christmas carriage.

But, today I'll just enjoy
the sun on my face

and smile knowing that
I owe this town,

big-time.

A Key to the Grove and Other Poems
~Peter Coe Verbica~

Coyotes in the Canyon
2009

At the devil's doorstep
once again
to pick up my daughters.

They're not answering the bell.

I sit in my car and wait
in front of a pale green rental house,
but don't ask me how long.

I'd be embarrassed
over such a simple question
and probably grin broadly,
before punching you in the face.

I hear coyotes yipping in the canyon.

It is out of context with
the uniform houses
of stick and stucco
near the University.

Two TV trucks are parked
at the Eastern entrance.

Finally,
something real to protest about:

a lack of money.

I'm having trouble writing lately.

I don't know if it's my cold fingers
or because I'm losing my mind.

Later, in the car
on the way to pizza,
we played a game:

my youngest would say a letter,
and we would think of places which
start with it.

During the fifth and sixth rounds,

a familiar amnesia
would settle upon me
as snug as a Panama hat:

and I would feel
as if my cell phone
had sucked out my soul

like a succubus.

When we came to "D"
someone had already
chosen "Delaware,"

and for the life of me
I couldn't remember Dubai or Dallas.

A Key to the Grove and Other Poems
~Peter Coe Verbica~

Dear Vanessa
2010

Dear Vanessa,

Busy with work
I thought that I had no time
to write you:

I have so many things
which I should be
getting done today.

I hear heels upon the
marble tiles at the office:

immaterial to most,
but to me torrents of sound:

sharp echoes
in the hall,

spooking away
the Inner Muse,

like a feral cat
which takes time to tame.

(Who has half a day

to walk with milk
sliding around a pie pan

under the noon sun,

and kneel in
a golden field of oat,
by a red barn,

just to wait for a Calico?)

How silly that I want
what I say to be perfect:

I realize that would
mean only silence.

And that is what I've given you
for many years,
too busy with work.

So, I am missing a meeting,
but in doing so, I get to
tell you that I miss you.

By the time I watched you
jump horses over fences,
you had already

jumped over the fence
of your youth.

And when you were young,

being pushed in a stroller
by an au pair,

reading a book in a swing,

making a school mission project,

A Key to the Grove and Other Poems
~Peter Coe Verbica~

or standing with your feet
pointed to
the edge of the ocean,

I didn't disturb you.

Now, I wish that I could
re-live one moment:

Just to ask, 'Let's take a walk
for a bit and tell me about
the book that you're reading.'

Perhaps then I could be more
a part of the beautiful novel
that you've become

and you wouldn't have to say,

"Dad, I don't understand
your poems,"

Because you would know
that I don't understand
them myself.

And, instead,

I could listen to you recite
from chapters
of who you are.

But, I know that this is but
a parent's unfulfilled dream,

and the reason why
as a grandparent some day,

perhaps I will have
the opportunity

to relive the moments
that I let slip by with you

when you were young.

Love always,

Dad

A Key to the Grove and Other Poems
~Peter Coe Verbica~

Joseph
2011

Joseph began inventing words
at the age of 50:

He was, now that I think about it in retrospect,
like a possessed carpenter
who needed to build his final house
for all of his children to gather after their diaspora.

Words to him were like wooden dowels:

they were to him what held
the pieces of things together.
And, to do this, they had to fit snugly.

Perhaps aptly, he invented a word
for the anguish one feels
when a family's home is sold
after parents die.

He described it as somewhat like
an optical illusion, reminding him of
two figures leaning together in conversation,

but with an artist's trickery:
the figures also transforming into
the eye sockets of a skull:

"I call this legerdemain a death
hidden within a death," he said,
or "deddentia."

He invented a word for the specific
inability to sleep at night
because of his being awakened as a child
in the early morning
by an immigrant mother with a whip.

She would beat out her anger on the world
through the red welts on her children's legs.

His insomnia was her epitaph.

Joseph said that this was "confusion within confusion,"
mostly from what came later from the lack of sleep:

the monsters which crossed through
the threshold of nightmares
and stumbled into the pale daylight
and stared at you in defiance.

He referred to this condition as
"monstrada" for the encompassing thoughts
which seeped through pavement
like lava and smoldered into the sea.

In nostalgic moments, Joseph would mourn
the loss of dreams let go of as a child,
like being a professional baseball player.

He likened this to an unnaturally rapid creep
of arthritis in the fingers,
when a painter, in a recurring devil's bargain,
trades his ox hair brushes one at a time
for seven cigarettes at dusk.

"I want to stand up in the movie of
these lives and yell, 'Don't do it!'" he confided.
"But instead I sit, quiet and tormented.
I am in the audience, but I, too, am one of the actors.
Do you catch this?"

He believed, like some medieval doctor,
that this pain wasn't harbored in the heart
so much as in the lungs,
because he found the grief labored his breathing.

This he described this as "evapoure," for
"it is when part of one's soul converts to steam and
ascends back to heaven to join other clouds."

Why he chose us to impart his wisdom
like a *sensei* didn't confound us then:
we were there, but unaware that he was a proud man
and held his mud to all but his pupils.

We were, in retrospect, his windows.

He said to us once, "I know these
things for an unadorned reason.
It is merely because I was born before you."

We only understood him synthetically at first,
until we grew older and had sorrows of our own.

"What feeling did you have the most

difficulty describing," I asked him once.

"That is easy to answer," he replied,
clearing his throat. "It was the feeling
inside of me when I discovered
that my soon-to-be wife was pregnant
with a child that wasn't mine.
But, I loved her so much that I didn't care and
wanted to be with her until I died."

When I asked him what he called that
feeling, he looked at me as if I had asked
the most ignorant question in the world
but he did his best not to show it.

"My son, that feeling is all around us...
and embodies unconditional love."

"But, what do you call it?" I asked,
still being young enough
to not be embarrassed by ignorant questions.

"I call it," his voice getting
smaller and smaller
like an adult reverting back to a child,
"I call it, 'Jesus.'"

A Key to the Grove and Other Poems
~Peter Coe Verbica~

Bare Hands
2011

I'm feeling flush,

spending 30 minutes
of my morning
like big banknotes

when I should be working.

The sound of raspy blues,
forlorn love, slow horns,
and a base beating

like a persistent
creditor's knock at the door
of America.

Notes from a piano:
brazen, anorexic, nonchalant:

take a catwalk
through the coffee shop.

I almost want to get up
and light the singer's cigarette:

tough to do since she died
over eight years ago:

on April 21, 2003.

All of this is a distraction:

like reading the
biography of a child prodigy
with three degrees,
a software sweatshop

and a kilo of stock options
cut with baby laxatives

chopped up on a mirror.

Don't look at me right now:

I'm like an addict
wearing a knit Peruvian hat,

fighting a battle
for my soul,

screaming down Back Bay alleys
at 6:15 am in the morning

and shaking my fists at
dead relatives and divorcees.

But you'd never know it,
because I'm smiling,

the smell of

A Key to the Grove and Other Poems
~Peter Coe Verbica~

ground coffee
and chocolate croissant:

and the sun unveiling
constellations of
water spots within the window.

I'm warming up in my sweater,
to the task at hand:

elbows on a round tabletop
of granite,

perhaps you've felt it:

that moment of focus,
when the crowd around you
blends into the background:

and you can begin to
create God with your bare hands.

I grew up
2012

I grew up with cattlemen
in the middle of a valley

at the end of a dead-end road:

They're long gone,
but I can still see them

through the dust,
casting their
dirt-and-diesel shadows

over the abandoned barns,
blacksmith shops,
and ramshackle ranch houses,

past the Eucalyptus trees,
oaks and sycamores

past the wood shakes
and weeping willows.

I earned my spurs with them,

dipped into the same
cans of Copenhagen.

I field-dressed wild boar
and dried brine-soaked strips

A Key to the Grove and Other Poems
~Peter Coe Verbica~

of beef in jerky houses with them.

And, I will salute them.

They're still

branding and ear-marking bawling calves.

They're still heading and heeling

steers in the hills to

treat them for pinkeye.

They're still mending barbed-wire fences,

and filling D-9 Cats with fuel:

on hallowed ground in my mind.

They're still swearing and
wearing their sweat-stained brims.

They're still spitting into the
palms of their hands

to put out their cigarettes.

(I can hear the sizzle:

it's like a cherry

held in the teeth
of my ear.)

They talk of tits and ass,
of boots and trucks and heifers,

of Labradors, Queensland heelers
and 30-30's.

This was years before

taxes broke the owners
like stubborn Mustangs,

before the city folk
came in like rustlers,
and bought up all the land,

before they ripped up this history
under a plow of mediocrity,

turning over clods in the dry ground,
for a crop of star thistle,

before the name of each ranch
was perverted to "open space"

and dedicated in
back-patting ceremonies
to termites, tar weed and
doe-eyed docents.

A Key to the Grove and Other Poems
~Peter Coe Verbica~

I grew up here:

where you learned
to roll out of a rabbit-punch,

and to shut up when you were told.

You learned to laugh
at the same drunken jokes,

but not to laugh too hard,

or the crazy-eyed joker
would turn on you,

fast and subtle,
like a rattler,

but without the warning:

and strike your jaw with
the back of a hand
which hit like a hammer.

I can hear them asking
for one last
hand of poker at
the bunkhouse dinner table.

I'll deal them in.

Every single last
one of them.

They're all in
for the final pot.

All of this happened,
in the pendulum
of summer after summer:

mowing through the months,
and leaving all of these memories
in a stream of rows

which looked as if they were
hand-painted upon the fields

with a pallet knife
chock-full of ochre:

Each story bound
in a bale,
wound with steel wire,

hauled onto a flatbed
in the heat,

and stacked into the loft
of one's mind,

to be fed off of later.

A Key to the Grove and Other Poems
~Peter Coe Verbica~

This is my library:

under walnut trees
which would canker

white-washed timbers
with black dots.

I grew up with these cowboys
who would admonish me
and say that

it's not safe
for a candy-assed boy:

you may never amount to much,
they would remind me,

and if you're not careful,
the world will be overrun

by doped-up hippies
and small-town hookers,

who will
screw you out of your
last dollar:

It's fluid in the lungs:
pneumonia in the middle
of a hot summer:

a jug of warm Sangria wine
nested in a tin-tub of
rolled oat-grain and molasses.

God save you from
the roughshod
of our ramblings,

they would confide,

they're worse
than being struck down
by lightening
in the middle
of a hayfield,

or getting kicked
square in the forehead
while shoeing a horse.

If years later,

you hear our musings scraping
under the braided rugs
in the ranch house of these lost decades,

take a shotgun to the floorboards
until you can get the little
bastards to stop.

Turn up the volume of the radio

A Key to the Grove and Other Poems
~Peter Coe Verbica~

in this tenement house in homage,
tune it to a Western song:

here, in the middle of nowhere, and
then walk past this plywood door.

Leave behind the rusted hay hooks
and cement sinks
and never come back.

How could they know how right they'd be?

How hard they would probably laugh
to know that the skinny kid
would be the last one to defend them,

and not let time cut off the testicles
of their memory:

to polish the German silver buckles
and Hamley saddles,
to remember their names
in black and white photos,

to stand up their statues,
in the real cowboy hall of fame.

Tombstone of a Town
2012

Imagine, if you will,
this tombstone of a town
where days lazily pass by,

as if each were
a white cloud sliding
across the bluest sky,

tracing an intermittent
shadow along
a barbed-wire lined road,

inviting a dog or a drunk
to chase it like a balloon:

this is the ghost, this is the phantom
of a lost afternoon:

This is a place where
a buck-toothed boy

drinks a soda pop
from a thick glass bottle
in front of the country store:

only to become the man
bent over a bar
in what seems like a single summer

(but actually takes six-and-a-half decades).

You may have talked with him:
the sound of his dreams

A Key to the Grove and Other Poems
~Peter Coe Verbica~

turning over and over

like the low whirring sound
of a tractor's engine that
someone hopes will finally start:

where an aged cowhand
with a big trophy buckle asked
him years ago

if he would
ever amount to much

and he never forgot.

There's a Polaroid of him
smiling with a four-pointer
stapled next to the tack room door
of the horse barn.

The date's written with a faded ballpoint pen.

That moment, if nothing else,
makes him worth something –
at least to me.

You are here:
at this former stagecoach stop,

in a truck that's too new
and gives you away as someone
who no longer belongs,

where you take refuge in the shade
so the heat of the day

doesn't burn the meat off of your bones,

where grass turns the color
of molten gold,

where you used to take refuge
in the winter

from the ice which
cracks the back
of the shale spine

which runs along these ridges.

And, when you're lying in a bed
in the old hotel,

your mind drying out like an orange rind:

you can almost hear the bawling
from the cattle cars which passed
through decades ago,

but you're not lonely because
you've brought along three familiar friends
for the ride through town:

a straw Stetson hat,
a snub-nosed, hammerless revolver
and a leather-bound King James' Bible.

You've come to pay your respects
and visit the house which you left
when you were thirteen:

there are more lines on its stucco face,

but you recognize
the Spanish-tiled roof, the windmill and iron
gates.

A diaspora of acorns are
scattered around
the trunks of the trees.

The weeds smell like licorice.

Everyone that you knew here,
rich and poor alike,
has long since passed.

A raven,
its black feathers ruffling in the hot wind,
watches

as you rub your wet eyes
with a fist.

You big, tough
cry-baby.

The Flakes
2012

The flakes, like snow in spring,
fail to show up.

I wait for them at a
warehouse turned coffee house
near the harbor of Hamburg.

It's a city of contradictions:

solar panels on roof tops
which blind the eyes of airline pilots
as they fly over,

energy-efficient concave windows
which melt the sides of nearby town homes,

windmills which act
like strobe lights
in the afternoon sun and

drive the heroin addicts in the park
into further delirium.

I've got the oldest tricks
in the book:

two sharpened pieces of
Titanium painted to
look like No. 2 pencils:

a grenade fashioned
in a bottle of beer that
could clear out the building and

A Key to the Grove and Other Poems
~Peter Coe Verbica~

a silenced semi auto pistol
with NATO issue

hidden in a pair of
conjoined paperbacks.

A secure smart phone
made smarter

with an embedded Geiger
counter adds to the intrigue.

I don't need to tell you
that I've alternated the rounds:

every hollow point followed
with an armor piercing bullet:

one for flesh, the other for metal:

it all comes out in the wash
with a tradesman's double-tap.

(I'd much rather be on the ranch
I grew up on, but such is the
destiny of pursuing a GI bill
education.)

There's a girl in a sun dress
with an anchor tattoo
near her elbow.

There are two
gay bikers with a gray bulldog

on a choke-chain:

And an industrial spy
noodling over his notes
on his view-restricted screen...

We all sit at different tables
but have a shared experience:

bad service, best endured
by tourists,

but harder to stomach for locals
like me.

Someday, I'll go to Lourdes to seek
a healing for my sins, but for now,

while waiting, I work on
solving a puzzle:

why no one reads *The New Yorker*
magazine anymore.

I surmise it's the font size: too small
for an aging demographic.

Or perhaps the smugness has worn
thin like a pair of black dress socks
which need replacing

now that so much uncertainty
is in the air:

with the disintegration of
the European Union looming...

A Key to the Grove and Other Poems
~Peter Coe Verbica~

I'm part of this:
my attention span lasts

long enough to wonder about
Teutonic apprenticeships
in austerity,

ironically preached during
their summer vacations...

I will confess to switching the sides
of my car to carbon fiber:

such is my fear of motorcycles
and magnet bombs...

I tip my hat to one
of the good guys
camouflaged in the crowd:

we're after bad men
on the wrong side
of a bright line:

and, I'll admit, there's
some comfort
in that...

The flakes:

I guess that I'll just have
to kill them at dinner.

Pants of the Dead
2012

We all put on the pants of the dead:
one leg at a time.

That doesn't make my visit to the mortuary
any easier,

a Brooklyn boy of nine shouldn't have to see

blue fingers, clouded eyes,
or purple-gray entrails
in a stainless steel bin.

Or hear the rasp of a bone saw
amplified by the hollow
of a rib cage.

(Even the crackle

of a Dodgers game
from one's home-made crystal radio

won't lull you to sleep
on the following night.)

So damn the critic who wants me to
imitate the poems of those
who have gone before me

and suggests that I read an anthology
which includes tales of pubescence
and flopping fish:

because, of course, the bastard's right.

A Key to the Grove and Other Poems
~Peter Coe Verbica~

They are good.

And though I would like to think
of him as just a grave robber

in a tie-dyed T-shirt,

I, too, have become intimate with
the cemetery.

And, I'll be damned if when you
hook up a battery to
the formaldehyde-soaked legs,

they do jump.

They do dance,

(even if they're just a collection
on a clothesline),

even if they're just
dead man's pants.

(Dedicated to Michael Weiner and Dennis Morton.)

Happy Birthday
2013

There, among shy shadows,
In between bony knees of trees. At the furry
Feet of mountains, a
Fire dances drunk on love in the breeze.
A dry-mouth man comes to water. A
New sun fills the sky, rising.
You are God's dawn and daughter.

Vanishing dewdrops like Sunday champagne
    on the tongue of summer - a sparkling tease.

A Key to the Grove and Other Poems
~*Peter Coe Verbica*~

© 2007 by Melissa West.

A Day of Ordinary Thinking
2013

God doesn't pity widows,
I imagine,

looking through
the Mission museum window bars.

The face of the largest Madonna
in the garden
blushes in the sun
with this revelation.

Why am I too cheap
to pay admission,

I wonder as I am taunted
by recordings of Gregorian chants

which wind their way
through the wood.

I smile and exchange pleasantries with a docent
working at the cash register.

Out of nervousness, I
photograph a wall of crucifixes.

I walk past the lean-to's,
which used to house Spanish soldiers,

the cacti fruit with their blooms and bristles,

the adobe half-walls.

A Key to the Grove and Other Poems
~Peter Coe Verbica~

I continue past the white-washed crosses
under a patchwork of branches.

Olive trees dance like Salome in the wind,
and for a moment, I lose my head.

You aren't with me to see

the statue of an Indian in rapture,
the mismatched and shaded pavers,
the mud and terra-cotta archways,
a family picnicking in the graveyard.

I notice that barn swallows have rebuilt
homes under the eaves.
I can see that prior generations of caretakers
knew to paint them blue,

but that this knowledge had faded away,

like words from a Latin mass.

It is the beauty of the open fields
which take me aback,
gilded and bronzed in the afternoon,

the beauty, but also the brutality,
as I notice a congregation of migrants
with bent backs,

picking berries.

I take a drink from a fountain,

leaning my head
over the drain as if it
is a moment on a silver platter.

There is life woven within the water:

There is the taste of iron
and the taste of earth,

but both are as shy as the Holy Ghost
and vanish in the heat.

The water twists like
a cool rope
until I turn off the spigot.

The hewn church doors are locked.
To be expected on a Saturday, I suppose,
but still, it saddens me.

Quintana and John are dead.
You had been married here,
in this little town,

which hides in the hills
like a forgotten sister
to more her more famous sibling Carmel.

Here, the wine is served in pitchers,
while slices of oranges
slowly seep in the red burgundy.

Only you could strike pose after pose
in an ill-fitting dress and pull it off.

Languid fingers,

A Key to the Grove and Other Poems
 ~Peter Coe Verbica~

you hold a cigarette,

your hand resting on a fence post,

at ease with New York City sycophants,
but all the while,

pining like a seasick priest
for the coast of California,

I realize,

after a day of ordinary thinking.

The Sidewalk Sale
2013

I have just recovered from the flu,

where you rejoice at no
longer having to wretch

bits of your soul
into a porcelain sink bowl,

where there remains
a raw, residual burn
in your lungs and throat,

and where woolen thoughts
keep you from shivering
in the heat of the afternoon.

My neighbor is having a sidewalk sale.

I can see the card tables from the window
of the converted garage next door,

in between the stunted palm trees,
patches of gravel and
skim-coated driveways.

Tubular wind chimes resonate periodically,
but I don't always notice.

I come after everyone has gone
(such is my fear of people)
to see what is left.

The array of things is an

A Key to the Grove and Other Poems
~Peter Coe Verbica~

unwitting autobiography.

I could name each item,
each mismatched, broken or incomplete piece

-- one after another --

but would that be fair?

It would just be me showing off
and in a way minimizing her.

I want to take a pellet gun to the seagulls
which seem to be laughing at her collection.

Anthropomorphic silliness.

I buy a broken trike
with rusted joints and rubber pedals
for three dollars.

I hand her a five and she puts it into
a yellowed business envelope, business-like.

She pulls out a couple of one dollar bills
and gives them to me.

I notice her swollen knuckles,
shaking fingers and
bags under her eyes.

I stand quietly
as the homeowner puts her vinyl albums
back into cardboard boxes.

I listen to her.

She talks about NYC and a favorite deli;

about her dad being lost
in the Pacific during WW II
and having to live with
her aunt and uncle in Indiana;

about her husband's fight
with prostate cancer before he died.

But, when she goes into
the death of her daughter,

while thumbing through
a children's book from the 1960's

(the one with the St. Bernard and boy
who race up steps all the way to heaven):

I am overwhelmed
with the need to leave.

I walk back barefoot,
rolling the tricycle errantly along the path.

Once inside my minimalist home,

I look with renewed awareness
at a dated picture of my four daughters.

It was taken at my ex-wife's half-sister's
wedding,

one of the last times we were all together.

A Key to the Grove and Other Poems
~Peter Coe Verbica~

"Stop crying or I'll really give you
something to cry about,"
my dad used to say,

his fist against my cheek,
pushing my head against the wall.

I add sage and other spices
to the chicken noodle soup
which is simmering.

Simple medicine to prevent you
from turning off the light in your own room,

simple medicine for those difficult days

when you can't seem to stand the sound
of even your own breathing

The Last Magazine
2013

It had grown so thin,
like a fortune from
a cookie,

like a blade of grass,
in my boney hands:

You could hold your
palms together with one
of the few glossy pages left:

as if to say what your
mind was on,

your thumbs pressed
beside each other

made the shape of
Virginia:

and if you blew between
the spaces, it made a shrill
whistle.

It was the Last Magazine,
with a feature story on
Apartheid

and a two-page
ad for designer sunglasses
modeled by Nadezhda.

Its printing coincided with

A Key to the Grove and Other Poems
~Peter Coe Verbica~

the same day as the
repeal of the Second Amendment,

which our Great Society
had finally outgrown.

I'll admit it was ironic when
they rounded us up.

We were unarmed,
but well-intentioned.

Without our Last Magazine,
we had nothing to read
or defend ourselves,

but hearing an announcement
over the speakers,

we took some komfort
knowing

that they would
round up and shoot
the poets first.

© 2007 by Melissa West.

A Key to the Grove and Other Poems
~Peter Coe Verbica~

Pilgrimage
2013

18 of my relatives
fly above
the Village

and look down.

The rain falls
into the violet mouths
of flowers.

The little goblets
fill to the brim,

quivering with silver,

stems shivering
with the weight.

A grandmother,
her daughters
and their children,

soar over the barns,
stables, goats,
stone fences and fjords.

Five small etchings,
three porcelain dolls,
a tongue-in-groove box
of family recipes,

a yellowing book

of poems by Njegos,
and, of course, atop a
wooden stand,

our family Bible

(with each marriage,
baptism, and birthday

carefully written
in Cyrillic
on the first eleven pages):

these things
are all that they
can carry

into the clouds.

Only God, the Devil
(and perhaps Chagall)
are there to watch
the miracle of their escape:

through the blackened chimneys
and melting windows,

as an orange oculus opens up
in the roof,

and they float into the sky,
like Orthodox prayers:

when the Nazis come
with their comical metal hats

A Key to the Grove and Other Poems
~Peter Coe Verbica~

and burn their big home down

with 18 of them
very much alive,

inside.

I guess that I understand better
why my grandfather
volunteered to go
back and fight.

(While there, he had a German
soldier bite off his finger
just before my grandfather
killed him.)

I guess now I know the
price of that WWII Luger,
the one he brought back and gave to
my dad.

It used to sit for years
inside his
bedroom dresser drawer,

along with a
slim container of
7.65mm Parabellum cartridges.

I sometimes wonder if
the red wine my grandfather
made in his cellar

and drank daily after working

in the mines

could ever quiet the rage
he must have felt,

knowing that his loved ones

were very much alive,
before the Nazis

came and burned down
their home

with 18 of them
inside.

A Key to the Grove and Other Poems
~Peter Coe Verbica~

Iron Woman
2013

The image comes to me
in stop-and-go traffic:

I see her in the basement,

carefully ironing her hate
into the clothes:

Her private space,

away from
the security cameras and
the senility of neighbors.

Her paintings from
college art classes
stacked like thin bones
in a cubby by
the dryer:

a secret catacomb.

The English Tudor house:

a bit too small to be
stately,

an orphan growing up
in the wrong neighborhood:

covered with inedible figs,
choking the drainpipes

with vines:

worried by
squirrels, possums,
and jays.

I remember a glass globe
from an investment bank
in the sun room:

hit by the hot afternoon
light.

It burned a line up
the wallpaper and
bore a hole

through an etching
of a schooner...

Outside,
an older blue Mercedes
coupe,
difficult to wedge the
car seats into and
later replaced
with something
more practical.

One more
God-damn party
to survive,

I imagine her thinking,

while I gazed

A Key to the Grove and Other Poems
~Peter Coe Verbica~

into the park across the street

watching soccer players.

Oblivious to the entropy.

It would take her 30 years
to escape the hell

and a decade after that

to wish she could
crawl comfortably back in.

When we first bought
the home,

the weeping willow
in the back yard

broke apart
shortly thereafter:

exposing a perfect family
of raccoons,

nested in the trunk.

The next morning,
I looked for their
alert eyes and
masked faces,

but they were gone:

an omen
of what was to come.

A Key to the Grove and Other Poems
~Peter Coe Verbica~

Happy Anniversary
2013

You eat the room
with your eyes,

ever so quickly,

like a caviar and
crème fraîche appetizer

on the sly.

Acting disinterested:

heavy eyeliner,
glossy-lipped,
and smoky-eyed.

It's heating up
inside you again,

barely kept in check
by the icy indigo
of your dress.

The music
harmonizes
under your sheer slip,

Your body can't help it:

the subtlest beckoning.

Your mind drifts to your cheerleader past and

a bus full of weeping boys
after a lost football game.

Your future:

a billionaire or two
in sporty cars,
sailing ships,

and daydreams in a red-tiled estate
overlooking Lake Como

with Botticelli's
"Madonna and Child
with Young Saint John
the Baptist"

under bullet-proof glass
in the marbled foyer,

just another painting
hidden
in plain sight
over a spray
of wild lilies.

A Cavalier King
Charles Spaniel
barks at his own echoes
in the hallway.

But, for now,
a group of
men rutting
at the bar in the tropics,

A Key to the Grove and Other Poems
~Peter Coe Verbica~

and the smell
of kerosene
from the torches

which wave to the beach
of night-blackened sand.

Your husband
brings you a drink
in a frosted glass:

a mojito
with mashed mint,
powdered sugar, soda water and a slug of
rum.

You respond
with a warm, sad smile.

Big, lovable, kind oaf:

How could he ever
understand,

that you have the power
to take this whole place
down:

with every wishful man inside:

and burn it to the ground.

© 2010 by Melissa West.

A Key to the Grove and Other Poems
~Peter Coe Verbica~

A Key to the Grove
2013

I couldn't write my way
across the river to the Grove,

where cares are burned away over a Lake,

etched under an owl's watchful eyes,

where a feeling of belonging
drapes over one's shoulders,

like an old leather hunting
coat, lined with
scotch flannel.

But a part of me is there,

nonetheless,
in the knowledge all of us have,

of human experience.

You don't have to
wait 25 years on
a list for that.

And if you peer hard enough
through the slats on the gate,

You might see it:

A bas relief emerges:

men's faces
carved into the dark
ebony of the night,

forming in a slightly
ethereal way:

like the faces and figures

which our imagination
creates in a cloud.

The bonfire illuminates
their cheekbones and foreheads,

and in their eyes,
a hint and harkening
of the boyish wonder

inside of them.

Greek mythology,
like the flaming bird itself,
keeps rising miraculously from its
own ashes.

All, a divine chiaroscuro.

But, today, I am
cross-town,
at the former
Pacific Exchange:

sitting like a Bechtel,

below the Spirit of California,

A Key to the Grove and Other Poems
~Peter Coe Verbica~

her giant hands full
of fruit, vegetables
and gold.

At rest,

on a stairway with wrought-iron scenes:

I think of my life as a stockbroker,
dandy, husband and dad,

the story of my life
wrapped and pounded into
polished brass.

My forefather first came here in 1848,

with a hunger in his belly,
and a single-action revolver at
his side,

to stake his claim
and dig nuggets from the
hills of Amador County.

I am important to him
as you are to your
ancestors.

Great or small,
we are precious,
lustrous testaments
to survival.

But, artfully slide
that filet aside

with the edge of
reality's axe,

and the true gristle is that

I will be forever grateful

that those towering
and ursine pioneers

who came before us

didn't eat all of their own cowering cubs

in the primitive competition
of life:

Otherwise, we wouldn't be here.

We would be a blink, a blank.

We would be interstitial.

The real trove is that despite the torrents and
droughts of time:

down a logger's
lonely path,

above a
buried buckboard,
crosscut saw
and riata

A Key to the Grove and Other Poems
~Peter Coe Verbica~

    at peace in shallow graves,

    past a root-ribbed
    box spring
    hiding in the fern
    and duff,

    amidst the morning's lingering woodsmoke,

    and under the stuttering alarms
     of a Steller's jay:

    There is the treasure of these cardinals,
    these sentinels,

    still standing in the Grove.

Beat by Beatniks
2013

"God bless,"

I say,

to the Wiccans,
hippies, and
part-time college
professors

who try to "spar with Beatnik ghosts."

That's what I say after
hearing their sneezes
first hand.

I'm in the first row
and wipe their snot
from my face.

I hate to say it,
but I think these

shadow-boxing
bastards

lose every round.

It's tough to win against the dead.

Especially when
they're so damned talented

that they wind up

A Key to the Grove and Other Poems
~Peter Coe Verbica~

rising from their graves

to kick your ass.

(By way of example:

we're still sitting
in our kitchen
with that
note-writing doctor,

who wrote right
over 1950 and 1960.

Years later,

we relish
with him

something
as simple as

a cold plum.)

Yes, I tip my hat to the
new shufflers
for stepping into the ring.

But, it's confirmed.
I'm a poet snob.

All of them
get called
out on the carpet
and bitch-slapped

by a brilliant barista:

Her art,

in "Day of the Dead"
woodblock-style
prints,

decorates
their humble pie
of a magazine.

Skeletons
hanging

on the backs of
pilgrims,

saint skulls
grinning,

and cars
flying into the
armpit of heaven:

the inverse images
soar above
the poems.

How can I tell these
writers,

"sparring against
Beatnik poets,"

that whether it's

A Key to the Grove and Other Poems
~Peter Coe Verbica~

music,
hunting,
or poetry,

you have to
have the courage,

the
unflinching willingness

to wait
for the pause:

even if it means

allowing your muse,
like a tarantula,

to nibble
on breadcrumbs

in your palm
of your hand.

We Could Talk
2013

We're a long way from
that day at the aquarium

where we laughed
at the kissing fish,

but we could talk
while we're
listening to
the stereo

or washing and
cleaning
out my car,

or on a run

to get some booze
and cigarettes
and stomped-on blow,

and some 3 am burritos.

We could talk
and drive around slowly,

kill five hours:
a death by hanging
around

under the cold sun's
first clean body shots
into the grey dawn glow.

A Key to the Grove and Other Poems
~Peter Coe Verbica~

We could witness
the street sweepers

totter and barrel and scream

as they
vacuum the veins
out of
Laurel leaves

which stick to
the wet pavement,

like a puzzle
of fragile fractals:

like a collage of
misshapen stars

which have fallen
upon the asphalt

of Los Angeles, CA.

Call it what it is:
our last picture show,
our skeleton dance.

We could talk
about that gathering
you wanted to go to:

where all of those people
convene in the desert

with clowns
and lights and
unicycles,

and chase a metal duck
car that shoots
flames out of
its head.

We could talk about
your wanting
to finish school,

or getting a full-time job
as a dental hygienist,

or whether you look
better as a blonde
or brunette,

or this dress or that
shoe or those earrings:

because I'm starting
to miss your
bewitching shadow

which used to descend down
our stairwell's walls

and disappear in
the parking lot.

I miss your outline in
the orange-red halogen

A Key to the Grove and Other Poems
~Peter Coe Verbica~

and your smoker's cough
in the morning.

How come you
left me a message

saying it's over,
to not call back,
and that I never
wanted to listen?

So stupid,
when we could talk

and watch
some TV together.

Before I got so
strung out,

so shaky and so thin,

when I used to
feel like a human being,

and hit the bricks
in the gym,

when we used to go
on walks together
along the shore:

we could have talked:

maybe about our lost baby.

(Your sister told
me about how she drove you
to the clinic,

with you crying under a
blanket in the back seat
of the car.

She swore me to silence,

and warned that she would tell you
about our sleeping together
when she was sixteen.)

But, now that you're gone,
I'm thinking,

if I could ever tear these
habits away,

like stitches
or staples from
my skin,

we could talk.

And, maybe
we could figure out
what was unspoken,

figure out
what was unseen,

like a warm waterfall,

A Key to the Grove and Other Poems
~Peter Coe Verbica~

or even a cheap hotel shower
washing over us,

and we could finally
come clean.

A Beautiful Ballerina
2013

Here I am,
on a red eye flight,

flying through
the darkness

after visiting you.

I'm just your dad
and you will always be my princess:

a beautiful ballerina.

(I don't mean this
with overwrought sentimentality.

Ballerinas
are anything but
soft or weak:

they carry the weight
of the world

on the sandpapered points
of their shoes.

The metamorphosis
from a caterpillar
to a butterfly is an
excruciating journey:

a dissolution

A Key to the Grove and Other Poems
~Peter Coe Verbica~

within a chrysalis,

an inelegant eating
of one's ego,

camouflaged behind
stage makeup.

I know that your effortlessness
is an apparition:

mastery paid for
with years of preparation:

It is the way of the
martial artist,
the marathon runner,
and the Olympian.

It is no different than
a mother's sacrifice
of herself.

Moments of brilliance
are your prolific prodigy.)

Memories
come back to me
from the soul
of this evening:

Under Midwestern stars,
cold wisps
of snow drift
off of the tin tops

of eighteen wheelers

on my way here.

I slow down,

wary of
the whiteout.

Buildings made from
blocks of grey stone

square their shoulders
and face each other
in the street

like bulldogs.

I hear the sound of ice
crunching under my radials as I park.

I lower my center of gravity
so that I don't slip as I walk
across the asphalt to will call:

to pick up the front row
 seat ticket you purchased for me.

(I hold it close to my heart,

as if I am an emissary carrying
a secret letter from the Pope.)

A gaggle of parents
and children merge
through tall doors.

A Key to the Grove and Other Poems
~Peter Coe Verbica~

It's an imposing Auditorium –
the largest theatre I've been in.

The main curtain
cascades for stories.

I gawk and then settle
close to the orchestra,
thanks to you.

I can read
the musical score
next to a celesta,

as it awaits to beckon
sugar plum fairies.

I see the violinists' bows
aloft,

ready to resurrect Tchaikovsky
and his friends:

(I recognize him,

mustache, beard
and eyebrows.)

He stands next to
the dutiful Ivanov
and Pepita,

who, as usual,
is showing off

his medals.

Dumas,

looking well-fed,
but regal in
his starched
French-cuffed shirt
and tuxedo,

weighs into
the conversation.

And, of course, Hoffmann,
ever the cad,

is present too:

always one step ahead
of a European war
or pupil's parent,

with his long sideburns
and licentious stare.

I sneak a clip
of you, as you
whirl across
the stage.

You are beaming,

despite the
finger-wagging of
your Polish
choreographer

A Key to the Grove and Other Poems
~Peter Coe Verbica~

who chides you
for smiling too much.

Tears well in my eyes
and I tether my emotions.

I freeze my hands on my knees.

I'm happy to be here!

I remember when
you were just a ginger snap,

full of mischief.

Who but you
would climb into our Koi pond,

like a big muddy fish,

all smiles in the water,
waving to your parents,

a turtle captured in your hand.

(I'll always remind you
how glad I am that
 I got to be a "party dad"
in the Christmas scene:

with you when you were
nine years old.

I set aside my shyness

and fear of dancing
to support you.

It was harder than loading
hay barns in the heat
of the summer.

It was a high dive
for me into
the water which is life.)

The big gestures on stage
remind me of farmers
sowing corn,

or peasants in a painting
slicing through wheat with scythes.

What could be more dignified than that?

As I write you,
I can hardly believe
the places you have been:

New York,
Boston,
Philadelphia,

Indianapolis,
Chicago,
Santa Cruz,

Belfast,
Panama City,
San Francisco:

and yet you are still
in your teens

(an age when I was
hoeing fire-breaks
around red barns,

roping polled Herefords,

and loading bales
onto the rusted back of
a flatbed truck.

I remember keeping pace

beside the dualies:

You never forget
the sensation

of dry grass and dirt clods
 crushing under your work boots.

Youth haunts us forever
in our dreams.)

A far cry from the cosmopolitan setting
you're a part of now:

the insider winks among
dancers dating dancers,

the tension of not slipping
on a stage wet with dry ice,

the subterfuge of
catching one's breath discretely

while fighting exhaustion
in front of an audience.

This poem is the small
bouquet I bring to
celebrate you.

I've folded it into
the back of a book,

hoping that you'll get
a chance to read it
again someday.

Just after your
mother and I divorced,

I came to visit you in Manhattan.

It was before I sold the
watch that I had given my
dad, so that I could pay
my rent.

You had dinner plans with
your mom and her friends,

and I wasn't invited.

So, I rented a
horse-drawn carriage
and rowboat
in Central Park.

A Key to the Grove and Other Poems
~Peter Coe Verbica~

I saw couples and families
and flashes
of color in the black and white,

and I can still recall

the sun on my face,
subtle smell of algae

and lapping of sound
as I glided across the pond.

I am glad that little boat didn't sink,

so heavy was my heart with sadness.

The Nutcracker story
is, in part, about fixing
those things
which are broken.

I will be praying for you

as your surgeon cuts
into your ankle

and repairs it
before the New Year.

I will take a
red eye flight
to see you:

carrying

Drosselmeyer's handkerchief itself
in my hands:

a talisman,
which for 121 years
has mended all
that is precious.

I know that your return
will be majestic.

No matter what lies ahead,
No matter what happens
in life,

know that
I'm just your dad
and you will always be my princess:

a beautiful ballerina.

A Road Trip Resolution
2013

A road trip resolution
borne

six weeks early:

inopportune
and not fully
fleshed out,

but we quit our day jobs
and went anyway:

leaving behind
the wet and sticky
bar floors

of Jersey:

Its flat-black paint
and glittered caverns

covered
with
peanut shells,
dried mucous,
pool chalk.

We left behind
the ghost blood
inside boiled egg
and vinegar jars

in exchange for
fresh air.

We wiped down
the tables
and cleaned up
the shot glasses

for each show:

with soapy
mop-water

and beer-fueled ruminations.

I can't say
it was pretty,

but the stack of weekly
newspapers,

lyric fragments
and
pilfered blues rhythms

written in pencil
on paper napkins,

the cigarette butts
with their lipstick kisses

lying
on brown lawns:

all were as free as love.

A Key to the Grove and Other Poems
~Peter Coe Verbica~

Our skull-heads
grinned and

we rode into the dawn
in a run-down bread van:

its diesel engine
as defiant,
as a silver-backed
gorilla

rattling the bars
of a zoo cage.

Children would laugh
and point at

the stuffed bear and mattress
tied down on our roof:

some would make fists
and pull down their arms,

trying to get us
to honk our horn,

which we did.

"Ahooga!"

We knew that we
were on a special mission,

like florists

who had to get all
of the flowers
delivered before

the end of a holiday.

We were trying to get
to California

by way of Yellowstone.

Our only wish:

that the magma underneath us wouldn't melt

our tires
and incinerate us,

along with our steel guitars
and steamer trunks
inside.

Steinbeck was nowhere
to be seen

when we got to Cannery Row.

The atmosphere
smelled of salt and fish.

We had 10,001 fliers
printed up,

crinkling them
over creosote
perspiration

and stapling them
to telephone poles,

slipping more under
the thin rubber strips

of windshield washer blades.

We managed to sell
5 cassette tapes for gas money

and sang theme songs
to reruns

on Hwy. 1,

all the way up
through Half Moon Bay
and Pacifica

to San Francisco.

That was 40 years ago,

when we were just the
opening act,

I've never
been happier.

And, now that
I look back
in the mirror

at my tattoos
and tear ducts,

perhaps never
sadder.

I guess that you've
figured out that I'm
famous...

Follow me downstairs:

I'm going
to make chocolate chip pancakes

for the grandkids and
crank carols up

full blast.

Rock and roll, baby.

Melissa West is an artist who lives in Santa Cruz, California. Nine of the prints shown in *A Key to the Grove and Other Poems* are from her linoleum block print series, *Camino de Santiago*. Her work has been featured in group and solo exhibitions throughout California, as well as various publications and a movie by Fox Searchlight Pictures. She received her B.A. in Studio Art from Mount Holyoke College, South Hadley, MA. To see more of her paintings and prints, go to www.mswest.com.

Peter Coe Verbica lives in Santa Cruz, California. He received his BA in English from Santa Clara University and a JD from Santa Clara University School of Law, as well as an MS from the Massachusetts Institute of Technology. He is married and has four daughters.

A Key to the Grove and Other Poems
~Peter Coe Verbica~

www.ingramcontent.com/pod-product-compliance
Lightning Source LLC
Chambersburg PA
CBHW060004100426
42740CB00010B/1394